SKH

FROM BLACK PSYCHOLOGY
TO THE SCIENCE OF BEING

DR. WADE IFÁGBEMÌ SÀNGÓDÁRE NOBLES

"Our eternal fight is for the
liberation of the African Spirit."

Dedication

To

William Edward Burghardt Du Bois

1868–1963

Frantz Fanon

1925–1961

Kimbwandende Kia Bunseki Fu-Kiau

1934–2013

Frances Cress Welsing

1935–2016

"For being the Doyens of our on-going liberation"

Skh: From Black Psychology to the Science of Being

Baba Dr. Wade Ifágbemì Sàngódáre Nobles

SKH: FROM BLACK PSYCHOLOGY TO THE SCIENCE OF BEING

Printed in the United States of America

23 24 25 26 27 10 9 8 7 6 5 4 3 2 1

Mailing/Submissions:
Universal Write Publications, LLC
421 8th Avenue, Suite 86
New York, NY 10116

Website: UWPBooks.com

ISBN: 978-1-942774-89-1

This book has been partially supported with a financial grant from Sage Publishing.

Contents

Foreword

". . . never be limited by other people's limited imaginations. . . .
The best way to make dreams come true is to wake up."

—Mae Jemison, MD, African American Engineer,
Physician, and NASA Astronaut

Knowledge is a puzzle that can confound the common intellect. The intricate pieces of facts, insights, principles, and data available in the universe of information must be placed together into a narrative that is coherent, comprehensive, compelling, and especially credible. These elements are crucial pieces of a tapestry that bind together distinct fragments of intellectual material into a broader conceptual template representing the assertion(s) being made, the theory being advanced, or the story being told. Such is the nature of authentic enlightenment and illumination. Work it out; solve the puzzle; apply the appropriate level of patience, ingenuity, sequencing, and just a touch of cultural texturizing; and the image one seeks to create is revealed, along with the satisfaction that comes from accomplishing that task. With this text, I invite each of you to read, absorb, and digest the latest from Dr. Wade W. Nobles, and those of us thirsty for elevated levels of enlightenment and illumination in the discipline of African psychology celebrate its publication.

The process dynamic involved in constructing puzzles also conjures up images for me of the ancient African Ancestors who revealed to us a formula characterized by a phenomenon I and others have referred to as a "building for eternity" (Parham et al., 2011; Hilliard, 1997). Having explored the great pyramid on the Giza plateau, walked the Temples of Dendera, Abydos, Philea, Komombo, and one built by the Pharaoh Ramses the Great in Abu Simbel, I have born witness to the hieroglyphics etched on the walls, the origins of psychology in the narratives, the genius of African Ancestors, and wondered how those ancient structures built thousands of years ago continue to be marvels in this contemporary time, while 30- to 50-year-old buildings and structures in the United States are regularly demolished or retrofitted.

Through further study and analysis, I have observed that the key elements the ancients embraced, among other things, included excellent preparation and construction on one hand and an aspiration to harmonize with divine intent on the other. This work, beginning with the chapter on The Advent, continuing with Finding the Skh, Skh: The Science of the Being, Culture as Restorative Technology, and concluding with Restorative Praxis Technologies is the essence of what "building for eternity" is all about. Dr. Nobles, as if inspired by that ancestral spirit and energy, expertly guides the reader through the intricacies of deep structured understanding of an authentic and genuine comprehension of the African-centered worldview. And just in case you might be a little confused, don't be. The aspiration and aim to harmonize with divine intent is anchored in Dr. Nobles's respect for the divine force in the universe, his love for his people, his commitment to excellence in study and scholarship, and his pledge to be the light from ancient and contemporary African spaces that continues to irradiate the true essence of our beingness as people of African descent who should know, understand, and embrace the spirit.

In the words on the following pages, I can hear Ancestor Baba Asa G. Hilliard III's voice, reinforcing to his friend and us all the need to "free your mind: return to the source." Indeed, whether helping the reader interpret ancient KMT philosophy, aligning with the Bantu-Congo conception of spirit and self-healing power articulated by Fu-Kiau (1991), replicating the self-determined posture of famed Ghanaian leader Kwame Nkrumah whose assertion of "forward ever-backward never" continues to reverberate in my own consciousness, or drawing on the Yoruba principles of body, spirit, and environment, Dr. Nobles has produced a masterpiece!

But so much information throughout history, especially within the discipline of psychology, when compiled and presented by those with less than honorable and, in many cases, scandalous intent, has skewed the narrative and presented a more obscure and baffling message to those seeking truth over lies, fact over fiction, and accuracy over delusion. I mean, just imagine trying to understand the human psyche without the requisite knowledge to recognize that "psyche" does not emanate from ancient Greece but ancient Kemet; that even theories traditional psychological theorists like Freud advanced, including the structure of personality and the psychic apparatus, show an interesting parallel to constructs articulated thousands of years before in the Nile Valley by the Kemetic people; and that psychology is not simply the study of the mind but the study of the soul or the spirit. Add to these observations the fact that it is difficult to trust and embrace any set of psychological theories or constructs that fundamentally do not support or affirm the humanity of African descent people, which is what Eurocentric and American psychology have done since their inception, and you have more than a justified reason to distrust and/or disregard that set of theories or concepts. Such is the fundamental flaw in traditional psychology and how it has been conceptualized, taught, researched, investigated, and practiced.

That is why this book is so important, not simply because, as Wade writes in the introduction about this text representing a divorce decree from Western hegemonic ways of thinking and doing, but because it presents each of us a road map forward to conceptualizing the essence of Black psychological thought. More importantly, it takes readers to places other texts in traditional psychology never go, even as he introduces to some and builds on prior knowledge for others the invisible world of spirit. Dr. Nobles also reminds us all in this intellectual treasure that understanding the essence of spirit is not simply a cognitive exercise but one that invites, if not demands, the use of sensation and perception as sentient beings capable of accessing and utilizing a full range of senses in coming to terms with what it means to be both truly conscious and human.

Historically, in reacting to these Western psychological notions of being and doing, much of the origins of contemporary Black psychology devoted time and attention to critiquing traditional psychology and its theorists because of these flaws. And well it should have in the spaces and times in which that work emerged, as the posture of "vindication and redemption" was adopted as a defiant and necessary strategy to soothe our assaulted sensibilities of people of African descent. Yet, even as the discipline of a more African-centered view of psychology has evolved, it has devoted substantial energy to explaining and describing what traditional psychology was not, and to a lesser extent, attention to what this science, art, and practice we refer to as a Black psychology actually was and is. Beyond his posture as a "healer," and in this space author, Wade Nobles assumes the role of a griot in this text adding depth to our understanding of how the classic works of Black scholars, intelligentsia, and revolutionary activists in early times and contemporary spaces, including Vastey (1823), Delany (1853), Du Bois (1903/2007), Woodson (1933/2033), Fanon (1961/2004), John Henrik Clark (1976), Diop (1974), Obenga (1992), and others set the stage for the development of theories advanced by Black psychologists post the late 1960s. The information in this text is almost encyclopedic in its coverage of "intellectual spheres/lineage in Black psychology," the Ancient Kemetic roots that ground our understanding of what those Ancestors believed to be our psychic nature, the conceptual reframing necessary to truly understand personhood within the realm of community versus solely as an individual, and the metaphysical understanding of spirit as the essence of all that is.

In the latter segments of this book, particularly in the chapter on the application of African American restorative technology, Dr. Nobles moves from the theoretical to the pragmatic in using not a digital application or device but cultural anchors as the means and mechanisms for aligning the human in us with an understanding of the nature, aim, and purpose of our creation, or beingness. Here, the reader can learn about how culture at the level of the deep structure, including assumptions about ontology (nature of reality), axiology (value system), cosmology (relationship to the Divine force in the universe), epistemology (system of knowing and interrogating what is truth), and praxis (system of and protocols for human interaction), are manifest in the ways of knowing and being. He also goes through the exercise of explaining his use of traditional African languages, helping the reader see how words have power and that power must be exercised responsibly in constructing our own theories and models.

These essential ingredients of this manuscript should provide both neophyte students to the discipline of Black psychology as well as experienced professionals alike with a conceptual grounding capable of bolstering their own academic instruction, counseling and clinical therapeutic practice, and program of research and scholarly activity. Reading this text, I suspect that you will feel as I do, that fortunately, our discipline of African psychology has come of age, and this manuscript, with all of its intellectual breadth and depth, is not only a great example of that reality, but a crowning achievement in a stellar career and body of work Wade W. Nobles continues to produce and leave us. Indeed, this text on *Skh: From Black Psychology to the Science of Being* is a legacy work!

An added feature of this book is Wade's implicit invitation to the reader to use this text as an intellectual, emotional, behavioral, and spiritual key that unlocks the shackles of conceptual incarceration that hold us imprisoned to the ideas of Western philosophical thought. There is no indictment of any of us who have been indoctrinated by the formal educations and degrees we have all received. Rather, the chapters in this text provide observations in the buffet of ideas and information that can help us avoid the intellectual indigestion and constipation that comes from consuming substances that are incompatible with healthy, life-affirming nutrition our minds, bodies, and spirits require.

In fact, some 37 years ago, Dr. Wade Nobles (1986a) was clear about this quest to find historical accuracy when he introduced the world of psychology and African/African American studies to the concept of "scientific colonialism," or the political control of knowledge and information. When characterized by three distinct but related elements of unsophisticated falsification, integrated modification, and conceptual incarceration, these components help the reader and learner develop a conceptual filter through which information one receives can be more appropriately strained, absorbed, processed, and understood at the level of the deep structure (rather than the surface structure), and used to fuel the behaviors that are a cause and consequence of one's thinking. The sharp mind and exquisite intellect Dr. Nobles possesses and wields are on full display in this text. His ability to take the reader to a plain that, for most, remains more latent versus visible is part of the aura that he brings. And yet, being a skilled academician and master teacher, he is able to walk the reader through content in a clear, understandable, and sequential fashion, even as he introduces the learner to new concepts and ideas.

In concluding this Foreword, I must also provide this footnote on what real character looks like in academia, and I make this statement having spent 40-plus years as an academician, clinician, scholar, consultant, administrator, and healer. Citing references from the great scholars of this and past days is an academic protocol followed by many authors and writers. That tradition is present in this text as well. Yet, make no mistake, while the citations throughout the book reinforce the principles and ideas presented in this text, this body of work is not an echo but an authoritative and credible voice. There is a fundamental difference, as prolific scholar and public intellectual Cornel West reminds us, between a voice and an echo. And in using his voice, Wade Nobles speaks purposely and authentically with an uncompromising clarity about the science of spirit and the origins of Black psychology. What I love about my brother and friend is that his voice is never tethered to an anchor of cautious reflection where words and phrases are constructed to appease those who tend to judge whether one's speech aligns with narratives external forces in Euro-American psychology believe should be socially acceptable. That has never been Dr. Nobles's way. And as he and I share a *Jegna*, a *Mzee* if you will, in the person of the great Dr. Joseph L. White, who instructed us both to never seek validation from one's oppressors, Joseph White is smiling from that ancestral plain where his spirit dwells, at this work Wade has produced.

But let me also invite you to authentically engage with it, and not yield to the temptation to be intimidated by the words, phrases, concepts, and ideas that are a part of this intellectual puzzle Dr. Nobles has produced. Rather, as with any puzzle, apply the appropriate level of patience, ingenuity, sequencing, and commitment to grow through the exercise of learning, and you will experience a level of intellectual, emotional, and spiritual satisfaction that will justify your journey through these pages.

Thomas A. Parham, PhD, President
California State University, Dominguez Hills
Distinguished Psychologist
Past President, Association of Black Psychologists

I

Introduction

My concluding chapter, Breaking the Code of Spirit(ness) and Consciousness, in *Seeking the Sakhu: Foundational Writings for an African Psychology* ended with the assertion that it was clear to me at that time (2006) that the epistemological dilemma faced by Black psychology was bound up in the inability of Black psychologists to truly understand the "invisible world of spirit" with models and concepts derived from our comprehension of the visible/material world. It seemed to me that a full and complete development or reascension of African psychology would require a language and logic driven by an explanation of spirit and consciousness—no less than the rescue and reclamation of the meaning of being human as spirit as the medium of human comprehension and understanding the *Skh*, the illumination of all.

It is important to note as introduction that sentient beings first became conscious of being conscious in Africa. African consciousness was the precursor to the idea of identity. While the ancient mind of prehistoric sentient beings is fundamental to consciousness and identity, this manuscript will not detail the many prehistoric discoveries and inventions, for example, imagination, curiosity, control of fire, dreaming, domesticating animals, use of thumb of prehistoric sentient beings. It will, however, accept the challenge to openly rescue, restore, and refine our ancient mind as grounding for the development of the science of Being, ergo, the Skh.

As an intellectual journey to the Skh, this book discusses the advent of the discipline of Black psychology and details its evolution to the Science of Being. With a brief critique of the inadequacy of the Western grand narrative, the "big ideas" essential to exploring the fundamental and necessary epistemic correction will include an explication of African (BaNtu) thought and worldview. It will detail the need to "return to the source" and explore BaNtu episteme as grounding. It will engage ancient African thought as both precursor to the modern appreciation of living systems (e.g., biophotons, quantum coherence, spontaneous biophotons signals, and squeezed state) and the science of Skh. Metaphorically, the text will wade in the ancient Nile River of thought, shower with the cool waters of traditional BaNtu peoples, and sunbathe in the thinking of Jacob Carruthers, Asa Hilliard, Kwame Nkrumah, and Audrey Lorde. This work is grounded in the African way of thinking, knowing, and doing as intellectual discourse. In proffering the application of African American cultural technology as the requisite for the restorative process, this manuscript also represents a divorce decree from the Western hegemonic stranglehold regarding the behavioral sciences. This journey concludes with illuminating the Science of Being and culture as restorative technology.

This book explores Black intellectual genealogy's trajectory as filtered through a timeline lens of before there were Black men and women in psychology to the advent of Black psychology as a discipline to its evolution as Skh: The Science of Being. In so doing, I most acknowledge that the technical tone of this book is due to the highly competent editorial acumen of the UWP team of Ayo Sekai, Geane de Lima, and Melanie Birdsall. I most acknowledge that whatever is profound and helpful resulting from this exploration is due to valuable interactions I have had with Naim Akbar, Kobi Kambon, Syed Kathib, Lawford L. Goddard, Joyce King, Maiga Hassimi Oumarou, Lewis King, Will Coleman, D. Phillip McGee, Marimba Ani, Edwin Nichols, Nathan Hare, Gerald West, Charles Thomas, Joe White, Robert Williams, Amos Wilson, Bobby Wright, Manoko Ratala, Daudi Azibo, Faye Belgrave, Nancy Boyd-Franklin, Wade Boykin, Edward Bruce Bynum, Kathleen Burlew, Patricia Canson-Griffith, William Cross, Dana Dennard, Babatunde Ife, Cheryl Grills, Jules Harrell, Janet Helms, Reginald Jones, Mawiyah Kambon, Harriett McAdoo, Carolyn Murray, Linda James Myers, Molefi K. Asante, Patricia Newton, Thomas Parham, Fred Phillips, Rachal Bayard-Cooks, Earlyne Piper-Mandy, Daryl Rowe, Margaret Beale Spencer, Jerome Taylor, Roberta Federico, Nsenga Warfield-Coppock, Tifase Webb-Msemaji, Adisa Ajamu, Mark Bolden, Kevin Cokley, Benson Cooke, Zethu Cakata, Anthony Browder, Kevin Bullard, Obádélé Kambon, Ingrid Goodman, Shelley Harrell, Helen Neville, Ezemenari Obasi, Jermaine Roberson, Maulana Karenga, Winnie Mokgobu, Davy Hay, Marcia Sutherland, Chalmer Thompson, Nancy Ewusie, Kaycee de west, Spencer Tyrus, Puleng Segala, Shawn Utsey, Kevin Washington, Evan Auguste, Derek Wilson, Abner Boyles III, De Reef Jamison, Shawn Bediako, Sharon Bethea, Theopia Jackson, Kenneth Monteiro, Patricia Nunley, Joniesha (JoJo) Hickson, Eryka Boyd, Jamila Codrington, M. Nicole Coleman, Tony Jackson, Erica McInnis, Lesiba Baloyi, Patrick

Delices, Natacha Pennycooke DeLoach, Daktari (Sheri) Hicks, Adanna Johnson, Brendesha Tynes, Kamilah Woodson, Ken Nunn, Huberta Jackson-Lowman, James Smalls, Emmanuel Tlou, Leonard (Dr. J.) Jeffries, Suzanne Randolph, Rameri R. Moukam, Serie McDougal, Ronke L. Tapp, Charlene Desir, Paul Altine, Guy Jenty, Georges Bossous, Floydeen Charles-Fridal, Fanya Jabouin, Oba T'Shaka, Erica Ponteen, Pascale Denis, Clancy Williams, Raymond Winbush, and Sonia Mills-Minster. Having personally sat with some and studied most of the following giants of intellegensia, it is a requisite responsibility that I acknowledge the critical influence of John Henrik Clarke, Ayi Kwei Armah, Ama Mazama, Djibril Niane, Ngugi wa Theong'o, Theophil Obenga, Moremba Kelsey, Chinua Achebe, Yosef Ben-Jochannan (Dr. Ben), Thabo Mbeki, Chinweizu Ibekwe, Letta Mouse, and Cheikh Anta Diop. In acknowledgment, I must also, as I have in previous publications, give special thanks to a group of Black men to whom I am related by blood and spirit. We started hanging out as teenagers and have grown to eldership together. As grown men, we met monthly (the 1st Friday) and talked, joked, teased, educated, and messed with each other. It is, I believe, the "invisible Ones" in heaven that sent through them a lot of "mess" that I received as special post hoc insights and valuable inspirations. Being able to sit in deep mess (caring and sharing) and learn from them is deserving of acknowledgment and I want to thank Fred Logan, Henry Nobles, Stan Sneed, Warren Sloan (postmortem), Paul Giles, William E. Cavil, Paul Logan (postmortem), and Ed Cotton. I must also thank and acknowledge my children (Michael Chikuya, Omar Jahmal, Zetha Awura, Ayanna Yasmeen, and Halima Bisa) and grandchildren (Talia, Mikal, Kristofer, Donovan, Johnathan, Deborah, Maasai, Afolarin, Moremi, Folasade, Yasmeen, Oni, and Zane) who I believe came from heaven to make their parents (me) mo Betta. And finally, I must acknowledge and thank my queen and life's gift, my woman, Dr. Iya Vera Winmilawe Nokwanda DeMoultrie Nobles. There is not a single intellectual scholarly thought, idea, or belief that I have expressed over the last 60 years that was not nurtured and filtered through the mindscape of her unlimited and boundless genius. She has consistently proven to me during our long and mysterious walking in the world that she truly "knows rivers and is deep as the waters." *Medasi Pa Pa Pa* Iya Vera with unending love and boundless devotion.

II

The Before

Modern Black psychology was informed by the "Vindicationist-Redemptionist Black Scholar/Activist" genealogy that started in the 1800s. The scholarship for the time was impressive. As foundational, one needs to only examine these writings: Vastey: *An Essay on the Causes of the Revolution and Civil Wars in Haiti* (1823); Easton: *A Treatise on the Intellectual Character and Civil and Political Condition of the Colored People of the United States* (1837); Pennington: *Text Book of the Origin and History of the Colored People* (1841); Walker: *The Appeal* (1840); Lewis: *Light and Truth* (1844); Holly: *A Vindication of the Capacity of the Negro Race for Self-Government* (1857); Brown: *The Black Man: His Antecedents, His Genius and His Achievements* (1863); Delany: *Principia of Ethnology: The Origins of Race and Color (Medu Netcher)* (1812); Blyden: *The Negro in Ancient History* (1832) and *Christianity, Islam and the Negro Race* (1859); Perry: *The Cushite or the Descendants of Ham* (1893); G. W. Williams: *History of the Negro Race in America, 1619–1880* (two volumes) (1887); Logan: *The African Background Outlined* (1936); B. T. Washington: *The Story of the Negro* (1909); Woodson: *The Journal of Negro History with Charles Wesley* (1916), *The Negro in Our History* (1922), *The Mis-education of the Negro* (1933), *The Association for the Study of Negro Life and History* (1945); Schomberg: *The Negro Digs Up His Past* (1925); Ferris: *The African Abroad: or His Evolution in Western Civilization: Tracing His Development under Caucasian Milieus* (1913); J. E. Bruce: *Concentration of Energy: Bruce Uses Plain Language in Emphasizing the Power of Organization* (1899), *Eminent Negroes* (children's book) (1910), *The Blood Red Record* (a history of lynching in the South) (1905), *The Blot of the Scutcheon—The Nation, the Law, the Citizen: Their Relation Each to the Other; No Heaven for the Black Man; The Black Sleuth*; and

W. E. B. Du Bois: *The Suppression of the Slave Trade* (1897), *The Philadelphia Negro* (1899), *The Souls of Black Folk* (1903), *The Negro* (1915), *Black Reconstruction* (1935), *Black Folk Then and Now* (1939), *The World and Africa* (1947).

Absent of the history of Western (Euro-American) psychology, at the turn of the century Black psychology's intellectual foundation was further grounded in the works of The Blyden Society—Harlem History Club: Hansberry, *Africa and Africans: As Seen by Classical Writers* (1977); J. G. Jackson, *An Introduction to African Civilization* (1937/2001); J. H. Clark, *Christopher Columbus and the African Holocaust* (1992), *Who Betrayed the African Revolution* (1993), *Boy Who Painted Christ Black* (1940), *Africa, Lost and Found with Richard More and Keith Baird, Notes for an African World Revolution: Africans at the Crossroads* (1992), *My Life in Search of Africa* (1999), *The African World Revolution* (1990); ben Jochannan, *Black Man of the Nile* (1972), *From the Nile Valley to the New World* (1991), *Science Invention and Technology: New Dimensions in African History with John Henrik Clark* (1991), *Cultural Genocide in the Black and African Studies Curriculum* (1972); Rogers, *Worlds Great Men of Color* (volumes 1 and 2) (1972); Williams, "The Destruction of Black Civilizations" (1974), *Rebirth of African Civilization* (1961); Houston, *The Wonderful Ethiopians of the Ancient Cushite Empire, Book I: Nations of the Cushite Empire: Marvelous Facts From Authentic Records, Wonderful Ethiopians* (1926/2013); Diop, *Cultural Unity of Black Africa* (1989), *The African Origins of Civilization* (1974), *Civilization and Barbarism, Precolonial Black Africa* (1981); Obenga, *African Philosophy: The Pharaonic Period: 2780–330 BC* (2004), *African Philosophy in World History* (1998), *Readings in Precolonial Central Africa: Texts and Documents* (1995); *Ancient Egypt and Black Africa* (1992).

As an intellectual journey and building on the intellectual genealogy of Black intellect, *Skh: From Black Psychology to the Science of Being* will detail the need to "return to the source" and explore BaNtu episteme as grounding. The journey will engage ancient African thought as both precursor to the modern appreciation of living systems (e.g., biophotons, quantum coherence, spontaneous biophotons signals, and squeezed state) and as foundational to the science of Skh. Metaphorically, the text will wade in the ancient Nile River of thought, shower under the cool waters of traditional BaNtu peoples, and sunbathe in the thinking of Jacob Carruthers, Asa Hilliard, Kwame Nkrumah, and Audrey Lorde.

In introducing culture as technology, it proffers the application of African American cultural technology as the requisite for the restorative process. This manuscript also represents a divorce decree from the Western hegemonic stranglehold regarding theory, treatment, and therapy in the behavioral sciences relative to African people.

This introduction regarding Skh and the Science of Being will first traverse the intellectual trajectory from W. E. B. Du Bois to Frantz Fanon and travel along the footsteps left by the Negritude poetics and politics of Leon Damas, Aimee Césaire, and Leopold Sengor. While the length of this discussion will not allow an in-depth review of the thinking of the Negritude poets, it is important to note the light their lamplights provided. The African American intellectual trajectory of Black psychology may best be captured by drawing a line between W. E. B. Du Bois and the Harlem Renaissance thinkers, the Negritude movement, and Frantz Fanon. W. E. B. Du Bois probably stands alone as the preeminent progenitor of the Harlem Renaissance. He and his work provided the philosophical foundation for both the Harlem Renaissance and the Negritude movement. As Rabaka (2015) notes, Du Bois's compendium of significant work[1] introduces themes that foreshadow the core concepts of the Negritude Movement. Du Bois's work literally places Africa and African people in the center of world history (Moses, 2008, p. 117).

As asserted by Rabaka (2015, p. 5), it is Du Bois's centering of Africa, his critique of racialization, colonization, and Europeanization of Africa and African peoples, and his participation in and legendary leadership of the Pan African movement that cement his significance for African American intelligencia and the African world. Du Bois's work is critical to understanding the enslavement of Africans in the new world and European imperial domination of most of the rest of the world. His scholarship and literary works highlight the consequence of race during what is called the age of Europe (1492 to 1945). Some have even said that Du Bois's immortal *The Souls of Black Folk* (1903) could be seen as the Rosetta stone and key to understanding the evolution of Africana intellectual tradition.

Marginalized in the broader field of sociology and social theory, Du Bois's experience and victimization by the indisputable double standard present in the White social sociological world and particularly the wider White world in general did little to destroy his fertile insights and may have, in fact, nurtured his innovative ideas that highlighted the beauty, poetry, and strange meaning of being Black, the vision and viciousness of the "veil," the dilemma of "double consciousness," the saga of "second sight," and the cruelty of life lived along the "color line." Written as a kind of candid self-reflection, Du Bois (2015) offered key concepts with an alluring preface that stated, "The blood of my fathers spoke through me and cast off the English restraint of my training and surroundings" (p. 255). The casting off idea can be seen as the birthright of Black psychology. Du Bois's contribution to the so-called solution to the sociology of race in *The Souls of Black Folk* revolved around the dilemmas and the dualities or the conundrums and complexities of what it means to be Black in the White world—what was commonly called, at the turn of the century, the

Negro Problem. It is Du Bois who noted that one of the consequences of White people's domination and their ability to normalize the ideology of Black invisibility was that Black folks began to internalize the "diabolical dialectic of white superiority and black inferiority." This, I believe, in turn, led to his conceptualization of the idea of "double consciousness." Du Bois further suggested that Black people needed to become critically aware of their "double consciousness" and how the utilization of White values and White culture as criteria for judging Black life worlds and Black life struggles was extremely insulting (impertinent) with respect to Black people's humanity, history, and culture.

While Du Bois was willing to work with White people who were honestly trying to overcome their prejudice and transgress their blindness to Black humanity, Black history, and Black worth, Du Bois was not willing to do so at the expense of downplaying or diminishing the physical and "psychological damage" that life behind the veil and living along the color line created. He also refused to accept the "diabolical dialectic" of White superiority, Black inferiority, and anti-Black racism and White supremacist misconceptions of Blacks and Blackness had on the souls of Black folks. As is often quoted, in his most widely commented passage in *The Souls of Black Folk*, Du Bois (1903) states that after

> the Egyptian and Indian the Greek and the Roman the Tuton and the Mongolian the Negro is sort of a seventh son, born with a veil and gifted with second sight in this American world—a world which yields him no true self-consciousness, but only lets him see himself through the revelation of the other world. It is a peculiar sensation this double consciousness, this sense of always looking at oneself through the eyes of others, of measuring one soul by the tape of a world that looks on in amused contempt and pity. One ever feels his twoness—an American, a Negro, Two souls, two thoughts, two unreconciled strivings; two warring ideals in one dark body, whose dogged strength alone keeps it from being torn asunder.

> The history of the American Negro is the history of this strife—this longing to attain self-conscious manhood, to merge his double self into a better and truer self. In this merging he wishes neither the older self to be lost. He would not Africanize America, for America has too much to teach the world and Africa. He would not bleach his Negro soul in the flood of white Americanism for he knows that Negro blood has a message for the world. He simply wishes to make it possible for a man to be both a Negro and an American, without being cursed or spit upon by his fellows, without having the doors of opportunity closed roughly to his face. (pp. 3–4)

This was a profound and revolutionary declaration that awakened Black intelligencia during that time.[2] During the 1920s and 1930s, young Black students and scholars primarily from France's colonies and territories assembled in Paris, where they were introduced to the writers of the Harlem Renaissance by two sisters. This significant act is an important event in history that gets little attention. Without the genius, activism, and inspiration of Paulette and Jane Nardal, the Continental and Diasporan intellectual trajectory would not have occurred.[3] The Nardal sisters owned the Clamart Salon, a tea-shop venue where the concept for La Revue du Monde Noir was conceived. Paulette Nardal and the Haitian Dr. Leo Sajou created this literary journal, published in English and French, that targeted African and Caribbean intellectuals in Paris. It was during this time that the Nardal sisters introduced the Harlem Renaissance ideas and thinkers to Césaire, Senghor, and Damas. The Harlem inspiration was shared by the parallel development of *negrismo* and acceptance of "double-apparentence" (double consciousness) in the Spanish-speaking Caribbean region. In a letter from February 1960, Senghor himself admitted the importance of the Nardal sisters, noting that "We were in contact with these black Americans during the years 1929–34 through Mademoiselle Paulette Nardall, who kept a literary salon where African Negroestrans, West Indians, and American Negroes used to get together." Jane Nardal's 1929 article "Internationalisme noir" predates by a decade Senghor's first critical theory piece "What the Black Man Contributes," published in 1939. The Nardal sisters and the importance of their Clamart Salon, as a conduit to the Harlem Renaissance, cannot be denied or minimized in the development of Negritude. The two Nardal sisters' contribution to the Afro-French intelligentsia's discussion and development of the philosophy of the Negritude movement was essential.

Frantz Fanon emerged out of, alongside, and beyond the Negritude movement. Fanon argued that those made "wretched of the earth" must rescue and reclaim their humanity and history from the "dark dank dungeons" that the racial colonizers had confined it to and to completely topple the racial colonized world. He boldly noted that the racially colonized must be mentally and physically prepared to violate the dividing line in social, political, cultural, physical, epistemological, and ethics that was imposed by the racial colonized. The break with Western thought, values, and beliefs (the midwife of Black psychology's birth) was essential to freeing the minds of the colonized. This, he believed, was fundamental if the wretched were to return to the upward path of their own culture and humanity. It is Du Bois's and Fanon's intellectual path and the "stream of thought" that they left that serve as the unacknowledged drinking gourd that nourished the evolution of modern Black psychology. Fanon alone epistemologically and praxeologically developed a critical theory of revolutionary decolonization that advocated for the need to embrace the use of counter ideology and episteme in order to rehumanize both the wretched of the earth and their racial colonizer (Rabaka, 2015, p. 320). Understanding the mental condition of African people was implied in the work of the Harlem Renaissance, the Haitian, and Negritude movements. It was Fanon who explicitly addresses the psychological impact of slavery and colonialism for both the colonized and colonizer. The ideas of Fanon captured in *Black Skins, White Mask* (2008); *A Dying Colonialism* (2022); *The Wretched of the Earth* (2004); and *Toward an African Revolution* (1988) should be seen as the mother's milk that nurtured Black psychology's break with White psychological thinking.

It is Fanon, the revolutionary psychiatrist, specifically who should be seen as the link to the evolution and advent of modern Black psychology.

From this multidisciplinary, Pan African perspective, there were, at the turn of the century and prior to the 1954 Supreme Court decision to overturn segregation, the co-presence of 32 early doctoral-level psychologists (see Guthrie, 2004, pp. 165–167) who were Black:

1. Francis Cecil Sumner, 1920, PhD from Clark University
2. Charles Henry Thompson, 1925, PhD in educational psychology from the University of Chicago
3. Albert Sidney Beckham, 1930, PhD from New York University
4. Robert Prentiss Daniel, 1932, PhD in educational psychology from Columbia University
5. Inez Beverly Prosser, 1933, PhD in educational psychology from the University of Cincinnati
6. Howard Hale Long, 1933, EdD in educational psychology from Harvard
7. Ruth Winifred Howard, 1934, PhD in psychology and child development from the University of Minnesota
8. Oran Wendle Eagleson, 1935, PhD from Indiana University
9. Martin David Jenkins, 1935, PhD from Northwestern University
10. Frank Theodore Wilson, 1937, PhD from Columbia University
11. Alberta Banner Turner, 1935, PhD in psychology from Ohio State University
12. John Henry Brodhead, 1937, EdD in educational psychology from Temple University
13. Carlton Benjamin Goodlett, 1938, PhD in psychology from the University of California at Berkeley
14. Carol Blanche Cotton, 1939, PhD from University of Chicago
15. James Duckery, 1939, University of Pennsylvania

16. Rose Butler Browne, 1939, Harvard University

17. Kenneth Bancroft Clark, 1940, PhD from Columbia University

18. Herman George Canady, 1941, Northwestern University

19. Frederick Payne Watts, 1941, PhD in clinical psychology from the University of Pennsylvania

20. James Thomas Morton Jr., 1942, PhD in psychology from Northwestern

21. James Arthur Bayton, 1943, PhD in psychology from the University of Pennsylvania

22. Mamie Phipps Clark, 1944, PhD in psychology from Columbia University

23. Shearley Oliver Roberts, 1944, PhD in child welfare (child development) and psychology from the University of Minnesota

24. Roger Kenton Williams, 1946, Pennsylvania State University

25. Howard Emery Wright, 1946, PhD in psychology from Ohio State University

26. Alonzo Davis, 1947, University of Minnesota

27. Mae Pullin Claytor, 1948, New York University

28. Mildred Mck. Statterville, 1948, University of California

29. George Thomas Kyle, 1949, New York University

30. Roderick Wellington Pugh, 1949, University of Chicago

31. Herman Hodge Long, 1949, University of Michigan

32. Montraville Isadore Claiborne, 1950, New York University

Francis Cecil Sumner, Inez Prosser, Carlton Goodlett, Alberta Banner Turner, George Herman Canady, and Kenneth Clark, however, deserve special, albeit brief, mention. Francis Cecil Sumner is believed to be the first Black PhD in psychology in 1920. He enrolled at Lincoln University in Pennsylvania in 1911 at the age of 15. At the age of 19, he graduated magna cum laude with special honors in English, Greek, Latin, modern languages, and philosophy. As a graduate student at Lincoln University, he taught psychology of religion, mysticism, rationalism, experimental psychology, social psychology, and intermediate and advanced German. This is in 1916 during the first World War. Sumner was an official translator for both the *Journal of Social Psychology* and the *Psychological Bulletin*, where he translated more than 3,000 articles from German, French, and Spanish. He was the head of the first psychology program in HBCU at Howard University. Francis Cecil Sumner's work on racial identity was essential in the case of *Brown v. Board of Education* (Topeka, Kansas). Inez Prosser was the first Black woman to receive a PhD in psychology in 1933. Her dissertation, the "Non-Academic Development of Negro Children in Mixed and Segregated Schools," for which she earned her PhD, was one of the first investigations into the social domain of Black elementary school children. Carlton Goodlett[4] received a PhD in psychology in 1938 at the University of California at Berkeley and an MD from Meharry Medical College in Tennessee. Dr. Goodlett and two other physicians were the only Black doctors in San Francisco in the 1940s. They were, however, only allowed to treat their patients outside the hospitals. Goodlett led a fight to win access for all Black doctors. In 1947, he spearheaded the fight against San Francisco's public transit for failing to hire Black workers. In 1935, Alberta Banner Turner was the first African American to receive a doctorate degree in psychology from Ohio State University. She was the founding president of the Columbus chapter and the first national program director of The Links Inc. Dr. Turner was instrumental in establishing the Prelude Scholarship and Recognition Program, a partnership of Links, Ohio State, and the Columbus Public Schools to honor minority students. George Herman Canady received a PhD in 1941 from Northwestern University. He was the first to study the race of the examiner as a possible source of bias in IQ testing. His master's thesis, "The Effects of Rapport on the IQ: A Study in Racial Psychology," criticized the neglect of the importance of the race of the examiner in establishing testing rapport and offered suggestions for establishing an adequate environment and subsequently became a historical treatise and a classic in its field. Dr. Kenneth Clark received his PhD in 1940 from Columbia University. He was a student of Francis Cecil Sumner. In 1954, Dr. Clark[5] and Isidor Chein wrote a brief whose purpose was to supply evidence in the *Brown v. Board of Education* case underlining the damaging effects racial segregation had on African American children. Dr. Clark also served as president of the APA from 1970 to 1971, where he promoted an ethic of social responsibility within the profession and confronted the institutional racism within the organization.

What is important to recognize and acknowledge is that there were Black intellectual scholar–activists who were addressing the mental condition and liberation of African people before there was the establishment of the formal discipline of psychology in America. This was the fertile ground that served as the garden patch for the advent of Black psychology.

It is somewhat miraculous that these Black men and women were even able to achieve doctoral status in an era of psychology that was shaped and nurtured by the "Western Grand Narrative" that supported a mindset grounded in ideations that White supremacy, privilege, individualism, difference, aristocracy, elitism, classism, racism, sexism, genetic inferiority, caste attribution and value, empiricism, and rationalism were the only ways to know and understand.

WHITE INTELLIGENCIA

Starting as far back as the 1700s, the White elite, in support of White supremacy, created a "thought prism" of false narratives, lies, and deceit regarding Africa and the meaning of being African that has polluted and contaminated all thinking and behavior toward African culture, people, and place in the world. Essentially nine "White Race Men" (Georg Wilhelm Frederick Hegel, Raymundo Nina de Gobineau, Cecil Rhodes, Flinders Petrie, James Breasted, George Reisner, G. Stanley Hall, Sigmund Freud, and Carl Jung) established the dehumanization, denigration, and inferiorization of Africa and African people. Their work, ideas, and opinions are ingrained in all Western educational and social behavioral sciences curricula and pedagogy.

From the early 1800s until this day, trends in Western psychology have emerged, declined, and reemerged. These historical trends range from *psychophysiology* with its emphasis at different times on "phrenology"; mind–body dualism, brain physiology, sensation, and hypnotism; to experimental psychology with emphasis on psychophysics, unconscious inference, scientific observation, Wundt's system, perception, apperception, and mental processes and laws; to modern psychology, with emphasis on content psychology, systematic psychology, animal psychology, evolutionary psychology, mental inheritance, educational psychology, Gestalt psychology, behaviorism, brain functioning, functional psychology, and dynamic psychology. Psychology, in all the different expressions, served as the scientific and academic expression of the Western Grand Narrative.

Guthrie's (1976) book, *Even the Rat Was White*, should be required reading for comprehensive examination in psychology. It provides us with by far the best overview of the problems and inadequacies of Western psychology. With regard to psychology and race, Guthrie points out that Western psychologists not only provided inaccurate data that led to racist conclusions, but that their behavior and conduct also called into question the intentions of psychological research. This latter point is very important. It may very well have been the "intentions" of Western psychology which necessitated the reascension of Black psychology. Is it unimaginable to suggest that the covert and in some instances overt "intention" of Western psychology has been to accept as true the inferiority of African peoples? The works of Western psychology must speak for themselves.

White Supremacist Intellegencia
Lying and Deception

Georg Wilhelm Friedrich Hegel
1770–1831

Raymundo Nina de Gobineau
1816–1882

G. Stanley Hall
1846–1924

Cecil Rhodes
1853–1902

Flinders Petrie
1853–1942

Sigmund Freud
1856–1939

James Breasted
1865–1935

George Reisner
1867–1942

Carl G. Jung
1875–1961

Images source: Wikimedia Commons.

Regarding African peoples, Western psychology in general accepted as a basic a priori assumption that African peoples were inferior. The conduct of Western psychology in fact proceeded as if this a priori assumption was a proven fact. It was probably no accident that shortly after the U.S. emancipation of enslaved Africans, Sir Francis Galton (1869) proposed the development and implementation of a "science of heredity" (i.e., eugenics). England's "good knight" believed that Black people were a race grossly inferior to "even the lowest of any White people." In 1869, Galton published his major work on "hereditary genius" and argued that, based on his "scientific scale of racial values," he was able to conclude that the average intellectual standard of the Negro was at least two grades below that of Whites. It is, of course, revealing that he chose to mention nothing of slavery, which ended in the United States less than four years prior to his "findings," as a factor in the discovered intellectual deficit. Galton, who was reportedly Charles Darwin's cousin, was adamant in promoting the idea of racial improvement through selective mating and sterilization of the "unfit." The acceptance of Galton's eugenic doctrine (c. 1860s) marks the point at which the natural inferiority of the African was accepted as a factor requiring no further proof by the scientific community. Galton's acceptance and promotion of the idea of eugenics were applied by Flinders Petrie, whose racist biases manifested themselves in his research on the material culture of Ancient Egypt. Most people aren't aware he was a proponent of eugenics, or selective breeding of humans to increase desirable traits. Herbert Spencer also greatly influenced the thinking of American psychology on this issue. Spencer, two years Galton's junior, coined the term *survival of the fittest* and developed the "doctrine of Social Darwinism." Spencer believed that the suffering of the poor was nature's mechanism for ensuring the survival of the fittest. In 1896 (cf. *Principles of Psychology*), he proposed that science be used to select the best character of the various inferior races and then breed them in scientific mixtures planned to salvage whatever rudimentary human worth was present. About 40 years later, Bache (1895) concluded that Africans were highly developed in physiological tasks and attributes. With a sample of only 11 African people and the prevailing scientific techniques for measuring "reaction time," he concluded that all Africans were highly developed in physiological tasks and attributes yet were slower being(s) in comparison to White on auditory, visual, and electrical reaction time. Parenthetically, the Bache research helped to inspire the Cambridge Anthropological Society to launch an expedition to New Guinea for the purpose of "measuring" psychological attributes of various races. The New Guinea experiments culminated in the St. Louis World's Fair experiments. At the fair, the World's Congress of Races convened many of America's prominent psychologists (e.g., R. S. Woodworth, later APA president) to "test" various Black African types. Despite the ceremonial atmosphere of the St. Louis World's Fair, these "scientists" were able to maintain the rigors of scientific investigation and, to no one's surprise, found that the darker-skinned participants rated lower in intelligence. In 1916, G. O. Ferguson, in a study conducted on the psychology of the Black man, offered the following prescription:

> Without great ability in the process of abstract thought, the negro is yet very capable in the sensory and motor power which are involved in manual work. An economy would indicate that training should be concentrated upon these capabilities which promise the best return for the educative effort expended. (Ferguson, 1916, p. 125)

Ferguson theorized that Black people were intelligent in proportion to the amount of White blood they possessed. He continued his attack on Black people by characterizing "defective morals as a negro trait." This statement caused other researchers to explore the moral attributes of other minority people. Edward L. Thorndike (1940), who served as president of the American Association for the Advancement of Science, and thought by many to be America's greatest psychologist, wrote in his book *Human Nature and the Social Order* that "The principle of eliminating bad genes is so thoroughly sound that almost any practice based on it is likely to do more good than harm" (p. 44). Nine years before he died, he completed his monument to American psychology and education (i.e., *Human Nature and the Social Order*) and offered 20 "principles of action" or "solutions" to the problems of human nature and the prevailing social order. The first and most important principle was "better genes" and, not surprisingly, he was an outspoken advocate of sterilization programs to "eliminate bad genes."

Western psychology as the scientific application of the Western Grand Narrative explicitly enshrined the belief that African peoples were representative of the degraded, deviant, demeaned, dehumanized, inferior, and wretched forms of humanity. In this regard, one can highlight the thoughts of the major architects (Freud, Jung, and Hall) of Euro-American psychology. Sigmund Freud (1856–1939) believed that African peoples held an inferior position to Whites on the evolutionary chain. Freud, though he belonged primarily to dynamic psychology, stands almost alone as representing the field of psychology. When we look at Freud's contributions, one is able to see, for example, that Freud simply built upon Greek thought and philosophy (particularly the Orphic mystery). Implicit in his analyses and theories are, for instance, the unquestionable acceptance of good and evil. The fundamental principle of Freudian psychology (Hall, 1954; Strachey, 1953) is that the structure of the "mind" is formed in childhood and that the child is a being with "needs." The "mechanism" which influenced or satisfied these needs developed by Freud stemmed directly from Greek mythology. The human possibilities implied in the Oedipus Rex tale of Greek mythology are demonstrative of the Greek influence on the psychology of Western psychology. For Freud, the Oedipal crisis was the chief structuring experience of the "psyche." The main feature of the Oedipal process was the child's sexual feelings of anxiety in relation to threats (against its genitals) by an omnipotent figure (i.e., the parents). Freud believed that this Oedipal process was universal. Freud's single influence cannot be denied. During his 60 years of active work, Freud singularly and sometimes personally influenced some of the greatest minds of Western psychology. However, without even a detailed elaboration of the Oedipal tale, one can see that, far from universal, the Oedipal myth is no more than one version of the original Orphic mystery in Greek mythology. Freud's recognition of the child's sexual feelings for the parent of the opposite sex is obviously related to Zeus fathering a son by his own daughter. Similarly, the "ambivalent feelings" can be viewed in the context of the Orphic duality of good and bad. Finally, the feelings of anxiety in relation to parental threats can be considered a modern-day version of identifying with the evil Titans. What is probably more relevant in Freudian psychoanalysis is that it represents evidence that remembrance of the Orphic story is embedded in the structure of the Western psyche. As a "victim" of that psychic structure, Freud was able to transfer the image of human destruction (the tale of the Titans) on to destruction of a part of a human (castration) and thereby resolve the personal anxiety invoked by his own theory. The real issue here was childhood sexuality and fear of castration. It expresses how Western theorists view the human psyche and whether or not that view is accurate or applicable to all peoples. Jung (1875–1961) believed that certain psychological maladies found among Americans were due to the presence of Black people in America. He noted that "The causes for the American energetic sexual repression can be found in the specific American complex, namely to living together with 'lower races, especially with Negroes'" (1950, p. 29). He went on to say that living together with "barbaric" races exerts a suggestive effect on the laboriously tamed instincts of the White race, and tends to pull it down. In his lecture to the Zurich Psychoanalytic Society in 1912, Jung (1950) spoke more fully on the psychology of the Negro and had this to say:

> The psychoses of Negroes are the same as those of White men. In milder cases the diagnosis is difficult because one is not sure whether one is dealing with superstition. Investigation is complicated by the fact that the Negro does not understand what one wants of him, and besides that is ignorant (does not know his age, has no idea of time). The Negro is extraordinarily religious: his concepts of God and Christ are very concrete. (p. 552)

Granville Stanley Hall (1846–1924) did not break with the tradition of his European predecessors. He, in fact, invited Freud and Jung to America. As the founding father of the American Psychological Association, Hall was also influenced by the Malthusian doctrine. His philosophy reflected the essence of the Machiavellian theory, which also deals with the dichotomy of White and Black. He believed, for example, that "what is true and good for one [i.e., the Caucasian and the African] is often false and bad for the other." If we were allowed to reflect on the period in history in which Hall was born, we would see, however, that he had reached adulthood before the American system of slavery was abolished. With this in mind, we realize that Hall had internalized the myths about racial inferiority, stupidity, and laziness regarding those of African ancestry. In fact, in a blatant justification for slavery, and possibly a counter position to the writing of a young Black sociologist named W. E. B. Du Bois, Hall (1905) published a treatise on "The Negro in Africa and America." In this work, Hall stated that

> Among the tribes of Dahomey, . . . and in the FOn, Felup Wolop, Kru, and other stirps . . . sometimes resort to cannibalism, use an agglutinative speech, believe profoundly in witchcraft, are lazy, improvident, imitative, fitful, passionate, affectionate, faithful, are devoted to music and rhythm and have always practiced slavery amongst themselves. (p. 3)

Hall goes on to state as fact that "polygamy is universal, fecundity is high and mortality great. Strong sex instincts are necessary to preserve the race. As soon as the child can go it alone, *it* begins to shift for itself. Stealing is universal and is a game and falsehoods are clever accomplishments" (p. 3). "Our slaves," he states, "came from the long narrow belt, not many miles from the sea. . . . It is surprising to see how few of the designated traits the Negro has lost, although many of them are modified" (p. 3). It was apparently the "intention" of White scholarship to demonstrate the actuality of its racially motivated or imaginary African American inferiority.

The intellectual atmosphere created by the anti-Black beliefs of the architects of Euro-American psychologists has heavily influenced Western psychology.[6]

THE APAS AGENTS OF HARM

Founded in 1893, the APA's Euro-American psychological lineage was nurtured by the mentalities of at least twenty-five philosopher-practitioners whose intellectual vision came into maturity at the height of America's slavocracy (see image on next page). Hence, the APA was nurtured with the "strange fruit" of America's pathogenic ideology of White supremacy. Its apology for doing harm, without restoration, seems impudent, hideous, revolting, a hollow mockery, fraudulent, and deceptive to even a nation of savages.

The White elite, in support of White supremacy, created a "thought prism" engrained in all Western educational curricula and pedagogy of false narratives, lies, and deceit regarding Africa and the meaning of being African that has polluted and contaminated all thinking and behavior toward African culture, people, and place in the world.

Disciplinary Heritage

Euro-American Psychology Intellectual Lineage

APA PRESIDENTS

Joseph Jastrow
1863–1944

Edmund C. Sanford
1959–1924

James McKeen Cattell
1860–1944

John B. Watson
1878–1958

B.F. Skinner
1904–1990

William Alanson White
1870–1937 ⊘

Jean Piaget
1896–1980 ⊘

John Dewey (APA)
1859–1952 ⊘

Arnold Gesell
1880–1961 ⊘

Paul Popenoe
1888–1979 ⊘

G. Stanley Hall (APA)
1844–1924 ⊘

William James (APA)
1842–1910 ⊘

Lewis Terman
1877–1956

Sandor Ferenczi
1873–1933 ⊘

Carl Rogers
1902–1987

Erik Erikson
1902–1994

Carl Jung
1875–1961 ⊘

Alfred Ellis
1913–2007

S. Freud
1856–1939 ⊘

Abraham Maslow
1908–1970

Alfred Adler
1870–1937

Kurt Lewin
1890–1947

Herbert Spencer
1820–1903

Franz Brentano
1838–1917 ⊘

Ernest Burke
1819–1892 ⊘

Karl Claus
1796–1864 ⊘

Herman Lotze
1817–1881 ⊘

Carl Stumpf
1948–1936 ⊘

Wilhelm Wundt
1832–1920 ⊘

Johannes Peter Muller
1801–1858 ⊘

Charles Darwin
1809–1882 ⊘

Alexander von Humboldt
John Herschel
Adam Sedgwick

⊘ **SLAVOCRACY GENERATION**
APA credited in 1892

During the height of the Black Power movement circa 1968, Euro-American psychology and the APA were charged with condoning the White racist character of American society and failing to provide models and programs conducive to solving African American problems stemming from the oppressive effects of American racism. A half century later, the APA issued an "apology"[7] decrying that body's complicit role in perpetuating White racism in society. It was stated that the American Psychological Association was complicit in contributing to systemic inequities, and hurt many through racism, racial discrimination, and denigration of people of color. Apologizing for being complicit in harming, undermining, and damaging the health and well-being of persons of African ancestry (both historically and contemporarily) is unacceptable. While the APA now asserts its desire to understand how psychology can meaningfully contribute to disarming and dismantling individual and systemic racism as a historical underpinning in White supremacy, in apologizing it fails to acknowledge its specific role in supporting structures of White privilege institutionally and structurally for centuries and its direct responsibility for perpetuating ideas, concepts, constructs, and theories that gave legitimacy to human savagery and inhumanity. Hence, by changing the skin you don't change the snake.

REGARDING REMEDIATION AND REPARATIONS

The APAs (American Psychological Association and American Psychiatric Association) as agents and arbiters of the field of Euro-American psychology should be charged with multiple counts of social, physical, and psychological harm related to (1) failing to oppose and/or support the invasion, kidnapping, torturing, maiming, trafficking, domination, dehumanizing, denigration of African culture, customs, and traditions (resulting in intentional miseducation) and attempted murder of African thought and beliefs was allowed, justified, condoned, perpetuated and in many instances directed by agents and/or advocates of White psychology and continues to perpetuate human atrocity in society globally; (2) contributing to a social atmosphere of anger, toxicity, violence, fear, hurt, hate, danger, damage, and destruction; (3) erroneous and consistent imposition of use of the term *psychology* as universal, which, in fact, is Euro-American psychology that is "indigenous" to the Euro-American sense of "Whiteness"; (4) serving as the scientific extension, explanation, and justification of the Western Grand Narrative of Black domination, negation, and nullification; (5) knowingly and historically justified and gave legitimacy to reification of Euro-American thought and beliefs as universal; (6) directly and/or indirectly contributed to and supported individual and state-supported acts and beliefs leading to the death and destruction of Black lives; (7) having an essential role in the defamation, slander, and libelous assault on the character, conduct, and consciousness of African people; (8) pretending to be arbiter of universal human functioning; (9) being complicit in, and not independent of, the torture and maltreatment of Black people by medical and psychiatric practitioners and establishment; (10) provided safe harbors to the practitioners of White supremacy by shrouding America's rabid caste system as a class and race problem; (11) acts of omission in supporting the profound and lingering psychological effect of global human trafficking, consistently referred to as "slavery," and colonialism has impacted the psyche of regular everyday African and Euro-American people; (12) providing and requiring foundational texts that serve to continually recruit, misorient, and validate the erroneous supremacist ideology within the required domain of "history and systems of psychology"; (13) supporting ideas and beliefs that minimized if not eliminated Black people's ability to attain those resources necessary to sustain and advance life and living; (14) failure to acknowledge its role in the defamation, slander, and libelous assault on the character, conduct, and consciousness of African people; (15) abdicate its unjustifiable claim to be the arbiter of universal human functioning; (16) failure to acknowledge that Euro-American psychology has been complicit in, and not independent of, the torture and maltreatment of Black people by medical and psychiatric practitioners and establishment; (17) failure to admit that its members and/or divisions have provided safe harbors to the practitioners of White supremacy by shrouding America's rabid caste system as a class and race problem; (18) failure to address how its support of the profound and lingering psychological effect of global human trafficking, consistently referred to as "slavery," and colonialism has impacted the psyche of regular everyday African and Euro-American people; (19) failure to recognize the historical legacy of foundational texts that serve to continually recruit, misorient, and validate this erroneous supremacist ideology within the required domain of "history and systems of psychology"; and (20) failed to examine the co-mingling of Whiteness, White privilege, and the pathology of White supremacy.

Given the seriousness of the APAs' complicity, there could be or needs to be a class action suit that translates the APA (as agents and arbiters of the field of Euro-American psychology) theories and ideas into loss of opportunities (education, political, employment, housing, health care, etc.) and to be made wretched (interiorization, negative, nothing, unwanted) for Black people while simultaneously advantaging White people. One should or could calculate for Black people who were wrongfully and intentionally diagnosed as mentally ill and thereby sentenced to various APA-approved and -certified mental institutions, for example, Crownsville State Hospital Psychiatric Hospital, formerly Hospital for the Negro Insane, the Ionia State Hospital for the Criminally Insane, the "loss of potential" and "being made wretched" in the form of education, health, behavioral (mental) health, unnecessary death, employment, housing and fairly compensated by the American Psychological Association and American Psychiatric Association.

ENDNOTES

1. cf, *The Suppression of African Slave Trade to the United States of America 1638 to 1870* (1895); *The Philadelphia Negro* (1899); *The Souls of Black Folk* (1903); John Brown (1903); *The Negro* (1915); *Dark Water: Voices from Within the Veil* (1920); *The Gift of Black Folk* (1924); *Africa, Its Geography, People and Products* (1930); *Africa Its Place in Modern History* (1930); *Black Reconstruction in America* (1860 to 1880) (1935); *Black Folk Then and Now: An Essay in the History and Sociology of the Negro Race* (1939); *Dusk of Dawn: An Essay Towards an Autobiography of the Negro Race Concept* (1940).

2. The Harlem Renaissance and the intellect of the Harlem Renaissance's writers, e.g., Langston Hughes, Richard Wright, Claude McKay, Alain Locke, as well as the Negritude poet-philosophers, e.g., Damas, Cesaire, Senghore, were nurtured by the thinking and concepts offered by W. E. B. Du Bois (i.e., "double-consciousness, the color line, White gaze").

3. *La Revue Du Monde Noir* was a periodical created and edited by Paulette and Jane Nardal in 1931 France. The publication ran for a course of 6 months and contained a wide variety of content including essays, short stories, and poems. A great deal of the articles were situated in the anti-imperialist, Negritude, and Harlem Renaissance movements.

4. As a footnote to history, Dr. Goodlet was my teacher and academic advisor at San Francisco State University (SFSU). Dr. Goodlett was arrested at SFSU in 1968 during protests by students demanding a Black studies department.

5. Dr. Clark along with his wife, Maimi, are best known for their 1940s' experiments using dolls to study children's attitudes about race. The Clarks testified as expert witnesses in *Briggs v. Elliott* (1952), one of five cases combined into *Brown v. Board of Education* (1954). The Clarks's work contributed to the ruling of the U.S. Supreme Court in which it determined that de jure racial segregation in public education was unconstitutional. Chief Justice Earl Warren wrote in the *Brown v. Board of Education* opinion, "To separate them from others of similar age and qualifications solely because of their race generates a feeling of inferiority as to their status in the community that may affect their hearts and minds in a way unlikely to ever be undone."

6. A fuller explication of Western psychology's inadequacies and views of African people can be found in *Bibliographic Essay* (Nobles, 1986).

7. While the APA now asserts its desire to understand how psychology can meaningfully contribute to disarming and dismantling individual and systemic racism as a historical underpinning in White supremacy, in apologizing, it fails to acknowledge its specific role in supporting structures of White privilege institutionally and structurally for centuries and its direct responsibility for the perpetuating ideas, concepts, constructs, and theories that gave legitimacy to human savagery and inhumanity. Hence, by changing the skin you don't change the snake.

III

The Advent

The advent of Black psychology represents a shift in the trajectory of psychologists who happen to be Black and a direct reaction to Euro-American psychology's racist underpinnings. As a real scientific revolution, it represented a critical challenge, critique, and correction of Euro-American (White) psychology and the intentional rescue, reclamation, and (re)construction of Ancient African Worldview and episteme. This was no less than a major paradigm[1] shift in the "thought universe." Part of this revolutionary paradigm shifting is the appreciation of the limitations and distortions resulting from blind acceptance of Euro-American psychology's universality and its hidden grounding in the Western Grand Narrative and White supremacy. What is essential to the Western Grand Narrative is the idea of a "linear hierarchical oppositional structure" that is the implicit legacy of the Western mindset as epistemic certainty (Dompere, 2006, pp. 54–57). Falsely accepted as universal, the idea of a "linear hierarchical oppositional structure" with Whiteness as its highest point is the core problematic in the quest to define, describe, and explain African notions of human functioning.

THE INTENTION OF WHITE SCHOLARSHIP

As noted above, the "intention" of White scholarship was to verify its grand narrative and scientifically demonstrate the actuality of its racially motivated or imaginary African American inferiority, that is, the diabolical dialectic.

The omission and miseducation regarding what it meant to be healthy and whole from an African-centered perspective inform the disorientation that many Black/African professionals experience and recognize as the limitations of their formal training in meeting the needs of the Black communities they serve. This results in unknowingly reverting to the Western Grand Narrative that in turn influences and shapes what Black scholar–practitioners see and accept as normal. Without intentionally giving primacy to African deep thought and wisdom traditions, what we know and have been taught, that is, Westernization, will cause us to automatically revert to White psychology by DEFAULT.[2] The danger of default is the "bellwether" notion that should serve as an internal predictor of seeing or calling an action or process African centered when, in actuality, one may have defaulted to a Euro-American action or process. In a very real sense, a direct consequence of the Western Grand Narrative for African people is that it infects the African mind with a disease that can best be symptomized as "Afrophobia," a persistent, abnormal, and irrational fear of things African; "Europhilia," a positive unwarranted feeling of love, liking, and affection for things European; and "Grecomania," a violent derangement of the mind due to Greek thought and ideas.

BLACK PSYCHOLOGY'S BIRTH

The Association of Black Psychology was born in the social, cultural, and political vortex of the civil rights and Black power movements occurring in the United States. The unending struggle of Black people from captivity and kidnapping from Africa to captivity and enslavement in early America to segregation and discrimination in contemporary times came to a head in the 1960s with the assassinations of our civil rights leaders like Malcolm X, Martin Luther King Jr., Medgar Evers, and Fred Hampton. Even though there were over 32 psychologists who were Black, Williams (2008) notes that, except for Kenneth Clark and Martin Jenkins, Black psychologists were virtually unknown. African American students and professional psychologists founded the Association of Black Psychologists (ABPsi) in San Francisco in 1968. The ABPsi was formed as a national organization free and independent of the American Psychological Association. In forming themselves, these Black psychologists who held positions in various academic, public, industrial, and governmental programs pledged themselves to the realization that they were Black people first and psychologists second. In the late 1960s, these men and women charged the American Psychological Association with condoning the White racist character of American society and failing to provide models and programs conducive to the solving of African American problems stemming from the oppressive effects of American racism. It is extremely important to point out and highlight that at that time, professional psychologists who were Black and students declared the primacy and importance of their Blackness over their status as psychologists.

In the now classic article in the *Journal of Black Psychology*, the emerging field was advised not to see Black psychology as the "darker dimension" of general psychology. Its unique status is derived not from the negative aspects of being Black in America, but rather from the positive features of basic African philosophy (Nobles, 1980, p. 23). It was stated then that Black psychology is the recognition and practice of a body of knowledge that is fundamentally different in origin, content, and direction than that recognized and practiced by Euro-American psychologists. As such, it was stated that African/Black psychology should be defined as a system of knowledge (philosophy, definitions, concepts, models, procedures, and practice) concerning the nature of the social universe from the perspective of African cosmology. What this definition means is that African/Black psychology is nothing more or less than the uncovering, articulation, operationalization, and application of the principles of the African reality structure relative to psychological phenomena. Akbar (2004) similarly defined Black psychology as a system of knowledge (philosophy, definitions, concepts, models, procedures, and practice) concerning the nature of the social universe from the perspective of African cosmology. Akbar (2004) further stated that Black psychology is not a thing, but a place—a view, a perspective, a way of observing. African psychology does not claim to be an exclusive body of knowledge, though a body of knowledge has and will continue to be generated from the place. It is a perspective that is lodged in the historical primacy of the human view from the land that is known as Africa (p. ix). During this time, circa 1980, the field was warned against a ghettoized and oppression-based conceptualization of African/Black psychology that focuses on the psychological consequences of being Black (Wilcox, 1971). Baldwin (1986) states, "African (Black) Psychology is defined as a system of knowledge (philosophy, definitions, concepts, models, procedures, and practice) concerning the nature of the social universe from the perspective of African Cosmology" (p. 241). As noted above, Baldwin (1986) believed that African/Black psychology is nothing more or less than the uncovering, articulation, operationalization, and application of the principles of the African reality structure relative to psychological phenomena.

Jamison (2018) concludes that the definitions offered by Nobles (1980), Baldwin (1986), and Akbar (2004) intentionally connect their articulations with Africa, deconstruct the victimization basis of African/Black psychology, and make a conceptual shift away from simply reacting to reclamation and revitalization. These definitions, he concludes, extend earlier definitions in that they address the cultural and theoretical basis for a developing body of literature in African/Black psychology that will continue to be produced, disseminated, and liberational. The Association of Black Psychologists (n.d.) formally defined Black psychology:

> African centered psychology (Africentric psychology) is a dynamic manifestation of unifying African principles, values, and traditions. It is the self-conscious "centering" of psychological analyses and applications in African reality, culture, and epistemology. African centered psychology

examines the process that allows for the Illumination and liberation of the Spirit. Relying on the principles of harmony within the universe as a natural order of existence, African centered psychology recognizes: the Spirit that permeates everything that is; the notion that everything in the universe is interconnected; the value that the collective is the most salient element of existence; and the idea that communal self-knowledge is the key to mental health. African psychology is ultimately concerned with understanding the systems of meaning of human beingness; features of human functioning; and, the restoration of normal/natural order to human development. African psychology is used to resolve personal and social problems and to promote optimal functioning with people of African ancestry.

INTELLECTUAL SPHERES/LINEAGE

Since the advent of Black psychology, Black psychologists have been researching and publishing in the attempt to find the authentic Black psychology narrative and voice. In so doing various, nonconflicting clusters of intellectual activity organically emerged as intellectual spheres or lineages. The mapping of the intellectual spheres was to create a kind of iconographic representation of the intellectual exchange and thought clusters happening with the birth of Black psychology and focused on the published members at that time. The attempt was to reflect the evolving mapping of the mindscape of the collective thinking of Black psychologists. In this intellectual geography, there are some places where there is a one-to-one influence, but for the most part, the thinking is best represented as clusters or spheres of intellectual dialogue and discourse which is more like stars or satellite clusters in our intellectual galaxy. Hence, there are atmospheric gravitational pulls between clusters, that is, intellectual exchange, or influence; stars that orbit together; and those that are naked to the eye (unacknowledged influence). In some places, the lines are drawn person to person and in some places (most cases) the attempt is to represent the directional cluster relationship with lines going into and out of a circle or cluster. These spheres represent teacher–student, institutional, and organizational collaborations. This spherical expression of Black psychology should not be thought of as competing schools of thought but more accurately as the nodes connecting an ever-growing spider's web representing the field of inquiry.

The decades of Black psychology writings and publications can be imaged as an interconnected cluster and lineage lines that resemble a webbing of ideas, theories, paradigms, frameworks, and models that have emerged from the urge to give voice to Black psychological thought. The mapping reflects the birth of the retention and invention of new noncompeting so-called schools of traditionalist, revisionist, and radical schools. It simultaneously and more accurately represents the growth of

Intellectual Spheres/Lineage in the Field of Black Psychology

Based on published work contributing to the development of Black Psychology.

27

the clusters of thought and theory and the pathways illustrating lineages that have sprung forth from the inspiration to be free of Euro-American hegemony and the independent search for Black psychology's African-centered core and essence. Historically, the evolution of the discipline of Black psychology engaged in the refutation, correction, and creation of ideas that were loosely framed as concepts, models, and theories.

BLACK PSYCHOLOGICAL THEORIES

A theory is generally seen as an explanation based on observation, experimentation, and reasoning (especially one that has been tested and confirmed), as a general principle helping to explain and predict phenomena, and a model being an approximation or simulation of some aspect of reality, which includes the most essential features or attributes of the phenomena. From its inception, the group of Black psychologists have attempted to not only correct and refute the damaging theories of Euro-American psychologists, but they have also created a rich reservoir of Black psychological theories about and by Black people.

The following critical theories related to Black psychology are worth interrogating:

- **Frantz Fanon**—Colonial dehumanization (*Wretched of the Earth*)
- **Frances Cress Welsing**—Cress theory of color confrontation (*The Isis Papers*)
- **Wade Nobles**—Extended self, shattered consciousness/fractured identity (*Sakhu Sheti: Foundational Writings . . .*)
- **Bobby Wright**—Mentacide (*Psychopathic Racial Personality*)
- **Naim Akbar**—Personality disorders (*Breaking the Chains of Psychological Slavery*)
- **Kobi Kambon**—Cultural misorientation (*Liberation Psychology*)
- **Amos Wilson**—History and culture (*The Falsification of Afrikan Consciousness: Eurocentric History, Psychiatry and the Politics of White Supremacy*)
- **Bob Williams**—Black Intelligence Test of Cultural Homogeneity [The Bitch Test] (*Ebonics: The True Language of Black Folks*)
- **Thomas Parham**—Counseling Blacks (*Counseling Persons of African Descent: Raising the Bar of Practitioner Competence*)
- **Linda James Myers**—Oneness model of human functioning (*Afrocentric World View: Introduction to an Optimal Psychology*)
- **William Cross**—Nigrescence (*The Negro to Black Conversion Experience*)

- *Daudi Azibo*—Azibo Nosology (African-Centered Psychology: Culture-Focusing for Multicultural Competence)

- James Coleman—(1969) Self-concept (components are self-image, self-identity, and self-ideal)

- Kevin Washington—PEST

- Michael Porter—Kill Them Before They Grow—Placement in Special Education

- Cheikh Anta Diop—Two cradle theory

- Tony Jackson—Slaying the Two-Headed Dragon

- Van Jones—The Reunited States

- Janice Hale-Benson—Learning While Black (*Learning While Black: Creating Educational Excellence for African American Children*)

- Anderson J. Franklin and Nancy Boyd-Franklin—Invisibility syndrome

- Boyd-Franklin and Nancy—(2000) The multisystem model

- Margaret Beale Spencer—Phenomenological Variant of the Ecological Systems Theory (PVEST)

- James Jones—(1991) TRIOS model

MAJOR ARCHITECTS

While the contributions of Akbar, Myers, Nobles, Phillips, Kambon, Grills, Hilliard, Parham, Boyd-Franklin, and Bynum should be viewed as some of the major architects of Black psychology, the list of architects is multigenerational and organic and ever-evolving. One can suggest that, generationally, the architects should include

> First Generation: Na'im Akbar, Kobi Kambon, Syed Katib, Lewis King, D. Phillip McGee, Edwin Nichols, Wade Nobles, Charles Thomas, Joe White, Robert Williams, Amos Wilson, and Bobby Wright

> Second Generation: Daudi Azibo, Faye Belgrave, Nancy Boyd-Franklin, Wade Boykin, Edward Bruce Bynum, Kathleen Burlew, Patricia Canson-Griffith, William Cross, Dana Dennard, Cheryl Grills, Jules Harrell, Janet Helms, Reginald Jones, Harriett McAdoo, Carolyn Murray, Linda James Myers, Patricia Newton, Thomas Parham, Fred Phillips, Earlyne Piper-Mandy, Daryl Rowe, Margaret Beale Spencer, Jerome Taylor, Nsenga Warfield-Coppock, and Tifase Webb-Msemaji

> Third Generation: Adisa Ajamu, Mark Bolden, Kevin Cokley, Benson Cooke, Shelley Harrell, Helen Neville, Ezemenari Obasi, Jermaine

Roberson, Marcie Sutherland, Chalmer Thompson, Spencer Tyrus, Shawn Utsey, Kevin Washington, Derek Wilson, and De Reef Jamison

Fourth Generation: Shawn Bediako, Sharon Bethea, Eryka Boyd, Jamila Codrington, M. Nicole Coleman, Chanté DeLoach, Adanna Johnson, Brendesha Tynes, and Kamilah Woodson

Fifth Generation: As the Sakhu Collective: Charlene Desir, Paul Altine, Guy Jenty, Georges Bossous, Fanya Jabouin, Erica Ponteen, Pascale Denis, and Elizabeth Louis

The caliber and complexity of Black psychology's reascension (Nobles, 1986) is, in part, due to the fact that it's birthing the critique and challenge to Western (Euro-American) psychology, was fundamental to the charge that Western (Euro-American) psychology denied, denigrated, or demeaned African American culture in its varied formulations of psychological theory and practice. As part of the critique of Western psychology, early Black psychologists were often in disagreement about what constituted Black psychology, what the nature of Black psychology is, and what should be the paradigm or grounding for Black psychology. Karenga (1993) classified Black psychology as having three perspectives or belonging to three schools. He suggested that there was a "Traditional School" that was mainly defensive, reactive to Euro-American psychology, and had little concern for or contribution to the development of a Black psychology. These Black psychologists continued support of the Euro-American model with minor changes and directed its work to change White attitudes. The traditionalists were essentially critical of Euro-American psychology without offering substantive corrective feedback. Karenga suggested that Black psychologists like Kenneth Clark, William Grier and Price Cobbs, and Alvin Poussaint were examples of the traditionalists. The second school was labeled as the "Reformist." Karenga believed that the reformist reflected a period in Black psychology's historical evolution and was embraced by some Black psychologists. The reformist Black psychologists maintained concern for White attitudes and behavior and used their work to focus on changing public policy. Black psychologists like Charles Thomas, Joe White, and William Cross were identified as reformists. The final school was identified as the "Radical School." The radical school made no appeal to White and directed its attention instead to Black people in terms of analyses, treatment, and transformation and insisted on developing a psychology that had its roots in an African worldview which was opposite to and different from the European worldview. Black psychologists like Na'im Akbar, Joseph Baldwin (Kobi Kazembe Kalongi Kambon), Linda James Myers, Wade Nobles (Ifagbemi Sangodare), Frances Cress Welsing, Amos Wilson, and Bobby Wright represented the radical school.

In a similar vein, Curtis Banks organized Black psychology methodo-logically. Banks suggested that some aspects of the field devoted itself to pointing out the flaws, errors, and inconsistencies in the Euro-American research knowledge base. These he identified as having a "deconstruc-tive" approach. Others in the field devoted their work to revising conventional Euro-American frameworks to reflect the Black perspective. He identified these as having a "reconstructive" approach. The final approach was identified as "constructive" where the work was being devoted to developing a new framework (paradigm) that is consistent with and predictable from the African American cultural substance. In 2004, I noted that African-centered psychology must address the cultural retentions and inventions found in African American life, especially folk sayings and proverbial speech.

AFRICAN-CENTERED/BLACK PSYCHOLOGY

In defining "centered" in Black psychology's evolution to African-centered psychology, I suggested that African centeredness represents a concept that categorizes a *"quality of thought and practice"* which is rooted in the cultural image and interest of people of African ancestry, and which represents and reflects the life experiences, history, and tradi-tions of people of African ancestry as the center of analyses (cf. Nobles [1998], p. 190). In expanding on this clarification, Rowe and Webb-Msemaji (2004) suggested that "centered" should not only reflect how the field should respond but the way it encapsulates the various efforts and perspectives being discussed as African-centered psychology. As reported by Goddard et al. (2020), Rowe and Webb-Msemaji strongly suggest that Black psychology practitioners should intentionally *locate* their theories, methods, and practices within the ever-deepening investi-gation into and reclamation of African cultural ways. As guidance, they suggest the following four criteria for assessing parameters of African-centered psychology. To be African centered should (1) utilize African cultural patterns and styles for understanding human behavior; (2) reflect the various ways African peoples have sought to understand, articulate, and project themselves to others and the world; (3) emphasize values that are more dynamic, circular, collective and situational, assumptions that are more integrative or "diunital," and methods that are more symbolic, affective, and metaphorical; and, (4) rely on African sources, such as oral literature (proverbs, songs, tales, and stories), praise songs and moral teachings, spiritual system, "scripts," prayers, and the dynamic interdependence of community, nature, and spirit.

Even before reaching this place, it was argued (Nobles, 1986a, p. 109) that the efforts to articulate African psychology were in flux, and as such, "the work we do is constantly changing and we continue to inform our efforts by the need to transform psychology. Current efforts should not be taken as an example of African/Black psychology being a complete or developed African/Black psychology. It is not complete. Most of the work of Black psychologists should be seen as African/Black psychology becoming" (Nobles, 1986a, p. 110).

In moving toward defining Black psychology as African centered, it was noted (Nobles, 1997) that African peoples' psychology is fundamentally derived from the nature of the African spirit and determined by the African spirit's manifestation as a unique historical and cultural experience. Akbar (2004, p. ix) in turn made the observation that traditional African psychology is "a place—a view, a perspective, a way of observing" and seeing humans as spirit, resilient, and capable of restoration. African-centered psychology would represent the self-consciousness centering of psychological analyses and applications in African realities, cultures, and epistemologies. It would include (1) a theory of human beingness, (2) a set of practices and processes aimed at connections, and (3) a system for determining and facilitating human functioning.

Accordingly, the idea of an African-centered psychology was being defined as a dynamic manifestation of unifying African principles, values, and traditions, that would have its own methodology based upon its peculiar approach to science. The fundamental tenets of African-centered/Black psychology are that Spirit is and permeates (defines) everything, everything in the multi(uni)verse is interconnected, the collective is the most salient element of existence, and all knowledge is communal self-knowledge. It was therein proposed that African-centered psychology, as a system of thought and action, would examine the processes that allow for the illumination and liberation of the Spirit. Dr. Thomas Parham, under the "jegnaship" of Dr. Joseph White, has not only raised the bar for what should be considered Pan African psychology in counseling, but his contributions, for example, *Psychological Storms: The African American Struggle for Identity*; *Counseling Persons of African Descent: Raising the Bar of Practitioner Competence*; *The Psychology of Blacks: Centering Our Perspectives in the African Consciousness,* have cemented the intellectual legitimacy of the African-centered thought in our discipline. African-centered psychology has been equally fortified by Dr. Cheryl Tawede Grills. Dr. Grills, the President's Professor, the People's Professor, demonstrated the exceptional value of Pan African psychology (Afrikan-centered Conceptualizations of Self and Consciousness; the Akan Model, African traditional medicine: Implications for African-centered approaches to healing, etc.) by "taking it to the streets." Through research applications with community-based organizations to assist in community organizing for social justice issues to clarifying COVID's impact on communities of color to California Reducing Disparities Project to the impact of the co-location of liquor stores, smoke shops, and marijuana dispensaries on Black and Brown communities' health and quality of life, Dr. Grills's work in Pan African psychology is indisputable proof of the value of intentionally utilizing and unifying African principles, values, and traditions as the epistemic lens for community engagement. The place of African-centered psychology, as a system of thought and action, has been the natural springboard for the illumination and liberation of the Spirit.

THE MOKO JUMBI STANCE

The Moko Jumbi (stilt walker) is being rescued and refined as an icon for symbolizing the dual task of African affirmation and decoloniality. The two legs of the Moko Jumbi are a good symbolic representation of the dual task of decolonizing the African mind and the affirming African beingness required in order to achieve "psychic reparation" and "social restoration." One leg (task) is charged with *the Affirmation of African Beingness,* the other leg with the *Decolonization of the African Mind.* In terms of decolonization, the task of freeing our minds (one leg) can be thought of as scaffolds or layers of mental experiences. These layers separately, together, and in combination with other experiences or activities help to remap the mental terrain of a decolonized mind. The experiences associated with or contributing to decolonization are (1) critical consciousness, wherein experience(s) can stimulate the reawakening from the amnesia resulting from hegemonic Western Grand Narrative, and (2) re-imagining the world wherein one is given the opportunity to draw upon a different episteme and thereby unleash the knowing of African Spiritness. This experience directly enables alternative and counterideological visions and fuels the imagination with alternative possibilities. Reconciling the intersect wherein one is tasked with the responsibility to create new understandings of the perceived "differences" (social categories, tendencies, etc.) as social constructions helps deconstruct or eliminate Western hegemony of thought.

In terms of the affirmation of African Being, the task of affirmation (one leg) requires the acceptance of the idea of being spirit and the notions of humanness and Pan African humanism as defined by African deep thought and wisdom traditions. From African deep thought and wisdom traditions and as defined in our ancestral memory, we are "Spirit Beings" and not human beings. As Spirit Beings, we are trifold, unfolding, vibrating, radiating energy/spirit (experience) of yet-to-live, living, and after-living spirit likened to a living sun, possessing a "knowing and knowable" spirit (energy or power) through which one has an enduring relationship with the total perceptible and ponderable universe. In living, we are concentrations of essence manifested for a particular purpose. We are Spirit Beings housed in physical containers while having a human experience. As after-living spirits, "We are the Ancestors." In material form, we are molecular concentrations (expressions) of the essence (energy fields) of our ancestors. In order to reclaim the African affirmation of Being, we must accept a fundamentally different meaning of being human and continually address the following specific tasks:

- Understand being Spirit (Divine Energy Made Manifest)
- Engage in both visible and invisible realms of reality
- Honor the feminine as primary and paramount
- Enhance the understanding of the sacred meaning of being human
- Advance human potential and unlimited possibility
- Provide opportunities for competence, consciousness, and confidence building
- Support cultural maturation and spiritual evolution
- Create life span development and transition rituals
- Invent rites of passage and achievement ceremonies
- Defend the right and responsibility to "walk in the world as a unique and valuable human being with an African face"
- Protect the cultural character of one's ancestral lineage and its contemporary unfolding
- Minimize personal trauma and shattering of consciousness
- Maximize an egalitarian lifestyle of proper nutrition, exercise, and spiritual evolution

In order to be "free agents" of our own "mental agency," to decolonize our minds, the following specific task must be achieved:

- Dismantle the edifice of Western (White) hegemony
- Deconstruct the implicit privileging of White thought
- Disrobe the false image of the White aesthetic
- Challenge and correct the singularity of a materialist ontology (linear polarities)
- Engage in the identification and elimination of "dehumanizing" systems, services, structures, and beliefs found in
  • Institutional oppression
  • Aristocracy

- Worldwide White supremacy and privilege
- Place
- Cultural denigration and appropriation
- Class privilege
- Racism
- Classism
- Sexism
- Colorism
- Elitism
- Political disenfranchisement
- Genetic inferiority
- Economic exploitation
- Apostolic authority
- Western educational pedagogy
- Chattel enslavement (thingafication and commodification)
- Patriarchal domination
- Dehumanization
- Menticide/epistimicide
- Caste (permanent attribution)
- Individualism
- Nation and state imposition

SHATTERED AFRICAN CONSCIOUSNESS AND FRACTURED BLACK IDENTITY

Arab-Euro-American psychological domination of Africa's mind can be understood as a clash of culture and consciousness. The clash is centered on the meaning of being human and the question of human relations, both of which can be illuminated by the utilization of a "memetic analysis." Dawkins (1989) defines "memes" as a unit of cultural inheritance that is naturally selected by virtue of its phenotypic consequence on the particular culture's own survival and replication. The meme itself is a unit of information residing in the brain. I have argued elsewhere (Nobles, 2012) that "memes" are "sensorial information structures" that are contagious information patterns that reproduce by symbiotically infecting human minds and altering their behavior, causing them to propagate certain patterns of behavior. Functionally, memes are any contagious information patterns, in the form of symbols, sounds, or movement, that are capable of being perceived by any of the senses and replicated by symbiotically entering the human being's "mind" and thus altering behavior in a way that propagates itself. Simplistically, therefore, a meme is an orienting idea that acts like a self-replicating nexus for the propagation and legitimacy of behavioral dispositions. "Contagious information pattern" can be summarized as or referred to as an orienting idea. A meme can be thought of as a unit of cultural discourse that, in influencing human consciousness, directs and determines meaning for the cultural agents who carry the meme (Piper-Mandy & Rowe, 2010). I have suggested (Nobles, 2012) that memes are "ideas which reflect the substance of behavior." As sensorial information structures, memes need to be able to transmit to the next generation their core content or meaning and capacity to preserve the altered behavior. The more fundamental the orienting idea embedded in the sensorial information structure is, the more it serves as a process of germination and, in effect, functions to influence the very process of knowing itself. These fundamental or foundational memes, in turn, serve as "epistemic memetic nodes," which shape and support a particular aesthetic, moral code, and set of human relations. The process by which sensorial-informational structures symbiotically infect the mind or consciousness, so as to reinforce or propagate the sensorial, is what I call "memetic ideation." Thus, one can classify types of consciousness or mentalities (e.g., slave/colonial mentality, Black consciousness, Franco/Anglophone, neo-colonialist) by defining the nature of the memetic cluster fundamental to its character. Memes or sensorial-informational structures can be in the form of ideas, symbols, images, feelings, words, customs, sounds, practices, or any other knowable and perceptible item or substance. Religion, political dogma, social philosophy or movements, aesthetics and artistic styles, traditions, customs, and every component of culture co-evolves and serves in symbiotic relationships as a meme complex. The integrated complex of culture can be seen as a "memetic ideation." The conceptual essence of a people's psyche is distorted when one begins to think in a cognitive way based on other people's schema. Rather than see ourselves in terms of the African tradition of the ontological principle of consubstantiation that says we are made equally, we begin to think that what makes us who we are, are those achieved attributes and characteristics. We think that because we have gained material wealth and status, we have also attained some higher level of being that requires that we separate ourselves from the common folks. For example, many can be heard to say, "I don't have to live in a so-called urban ghetto anymore because I have money; therefore, I am better than the rest of 'them'"; or "I have been to school in America or Europe and therefore I am better than these 'natives'." Accordingly, both continental and diasporan consciousness and identity reflect limitations in the African ability to think in a way that is congruent with the kaleidoscope and gumbo of an African epistemological worldview.

The intentional destruction of the African mind was to shatter African consciousness and fracture Black identity for both continental and diasporic Africans throughout the world. The importance of violence in the shattering of African consciousness and fracturing of Black identity comes out of the work of Fanon (2008), who makes the point that there are forms of violence that are destructive to the spirit of African people. His work notes different types of violence, for example, raw vulgar violence, historical violence, and violence beyond violence. Historical violence, he pointed out, is historical destruction that occurs when people are subjected to destruction, plundering, vandalization, to false systems of pacification. Fanon talked about a level of violence beyond violence. He said this is the invisible destructive force that is always at work, which expresses itself as an alien form of universal values and dominant norms. When Europe proposes its system of values and norms as universal, it becomes violence beyond violence. This kind of violence is invisible. You are not able to see it or detect it as strange. Violence beyond violence is a compelling and dangerously frightening phenomenon. It is the cause of rupture in one's psyche. As such, we simply continue the process of being victims of the psychology of violence and never knowing that we are the victims. Within the devastation of the violence beyond violence, we don't see the many acts of ethno-cultural genocide. We don't need to see it because the psychology of violence beyond violence is so subtle that we feel blessed that we escaped, that we got away, that we are still alive, that we ain't like the rest of the niggas. It is intellectually painful to even contemplate or think with a ruptured psyche, and it is even more painful to recognize the intellectual disability in conceptualizing the extent of the damage. One must ultimately recognize the worldwide historical and contemporary processes that were designed to destroy or disrupt the human meaning of being African. The historical enslavement and contemporary exploitation of African people could only be successful if the African meanings of being human were erased or redefined. If and only when the African meanings of being human are removed from the center (ergo, Afrocentricity) of African people's consciousness can African people be permanently enslaved. This process of shattering African consciousness and fracturing Black identity is the key lingering effect of the enslavement process. It was (is), in fact, a worldwide phenomenon integrally bound to the process of "Westernization." In this regard, the experience of Africans everywhere in the Diaspora was formulaic.

In order to illustrate the pervasive and debilitating power of shattering African consciousness and fracturing Black identity, I have utilized the idea of memes (Nobles, 2013) and the capacity of memetic infections to alter behavior which propagates the destructive pattern embedded in the meaning coded in the memetic idea. As noted, a Meme or Sensoria-Information Structure is any contagious information pattern that replicates by symbiotically infecting human minds and altering their behaviors, causing them to propagate the pattern. These Sensoria-Information Structures can be in the form of symbols, images, feelings, words, ideas, customs, practices, or any knowable and perceptible item or substance. As sensorial information structures, memes are "passed on" from one generation to the next while preserving their core content or meaning and capacity to preserve the altered behavior. Memetics would, in fact, suggest that the contagious information pattern that replicated itself via infecting the mind of the enslaved African was an identifiable complex of ideas and experiences that supported the belief that the African was "chattel" and void of human value and worth. Clearly shattered African consciousness and fractured Black identity resulting from enslavement and colonization's aftermath persist in the forms of White supremacy, cultural domination, and identity confusion throughout the world today. It was and is an important determinant in the psychological development of African people in the Americas: North America (e.g., U.S.), Central America (e.g., Mexico), South America (e.g., Brazil), and the West Indies (e.g., Cuba) and Africa.

In order to better frame the discourse, several concepts and constructs will be presented as guidelines for analyses and interpretation. The concepts of consciousness and identity, experiential communality, extended self, scientific colonialism, transubstantiation, and the notion of spirit person all will be used to revisit and further frame the discussion of the lingering effects of the enslavement era.

> Conceptual Incarceration: The state of conceptual incarceration inhibits the African thinker from asking the right questions and developing an authentic theory. We are limited in what we can know about African social reality by what we think we know about the dynamics of social reality in general (an understanding which is guided by the ideological premise of another people's science). This epistemological dilemma for African social scientists is that we find ourselves seeking an awareness and understanding of our own reality, yet the parameters of the definition of what constitutes knowledge about reality (i.e., the ideological base of science) is defined according to non-Black conception.

The Africans who were sold, kidnapped, or stolen and brought to the Americas had to make sense of or give meaning to the reality of a new place, status, and people. Despite the derailment, the only "mental map" that was available for them to navigate and give meaning to the new condition of bondage and barbarism was the mental map of being African. Domination infects (memetic infection) those oppressed or enslaved with a punishing "superego" that excludes and abjects them. The result is that "desire" itself becomes split and fragmented, and the legacy of enslavement creates a consciousness that simultaneously includes a terrifying memetic cluster of objectification that is included by the dominant superego that is being embraced or adopted. The introjection of this superego or alien consciousness necessarily creates a sense of debilitating anti-self-consciousness, which at its extreme can be akin to internal "voices" heard by people with schizophrenia.[3] The perverse consciousness commands self-negation and nullification that undermines the seat of wellness and agency. Domination and racist dehumanization memetically infect the mind and consciousness of those made wretched (oppressed) with a fractured consciousness and shattered identity whose memetic composition is overwhelmed with anti-African ideas and the negation of Blackness such that African/Black consciousness excludes and abjects the sense of being human. This memetic infection creates a pathological sense of alienation from humanity far more severe than the Dubosian idea of double consciousness or the Oliverian notion of double alienation. In this mental state, the very meaning of being and the act of thinking about "doing" is filled with memetic ideations that are antagonistic to one's value and meaning of being human.

The legacy of chattel slavery has, in fact, placed the proper understanding of the African American experience in a cauldron of unaddressed Black and White pathology. The pathology of White supremacy has resulted in an unabated set of assumptions and beliefs that conceive African American reality as simply expressions of human deviancy stemming from, at best, socially determined deficits or, at worse, genetically defined inadequacies absent of any sense of cultural integrity.[4]

Continuing to walk in this place represents the attempt to "find the Skh."

ENDNOTES

1. A paradigm serves as the formalized framework that guides the assessment and evaluation of reality. The paradigm is, in effect, the perceptual, cognitive, and affective achievement representing the organizational plan for thinking, feeling, understanding, and doing. The paradigm is a comprehensive model of understanding that establishes viewpoints and rules on how one understands reality and identifies problems and how to solve them. In effect, the paradigm identifies what is to be observed and scrutinized; the kind of questions that are supposed to be asked and probed for answers in relation to a subject; how the investigation and explorations are to be structured; and how the results (outcomes) should be interpreted. The Western Grand Narrative should be understood as being part of a constructive process in which Euro-American people interpret and reinterpret their experiences as reflections of

their deep intrinsic beliefs as both descriptive and explanative discourse. Euro-American people use their epistemic reflections, cultural appreciations, and apperceptions about reality to inform their knowing framework and intellectual mindsets to further recognize and record the making of sense of events and experiences as a grand narrative. In effect, the paradigm binds, shapes, dictates, and determines all other conceptual tools like indigeneity, orthodoxy, theory, therapy, and research. Paradigm shifting should reflect the adoption and utilization of "language" that represents and reflects the new thinking and doing. The importance of "languaging" is fundamental.

2. The idea of default is important. To default is to fail to complete the full due or to return to that which is insufficient. In this regard, the recognition that without intentionally giving primacy to African deep thought and wisdom traditions, what we know and have been taught, that is, Westernization, will cause us to automatically revert back to White psychology by DEFAULT as translation. The danger of default should become a "bellwether" notion that serves as an internal predictor for seeing or calling an action or process African centered when, in actuality, it was Euro-American.

3. The hunting White superego of a White supremacist culture, in the form of memetic clusters infecting consciousness, may be misdiagnosed as schizophrenia in Black people.

4. Too often the perceived absence of indigenous language leads to the belief that there is also the absence of culture.

IV

Finding the Skh

The historical aim of Black psychology was (is) to extricate ourselves from the limitations of the language and metaphors of Eurocentric psychology and to establish a distinct "place" for African realities to rest. In directing us to locate Africa's cultural unity in its language, history, and psyche, Diop, unfortunately, left the exploration of the psychic unity undone.

In guarding the shifting process, we offered as a guide the Yoruba adage *Idale wa ninu titumo ede,* meaning that treachery is in the translation. In paradigm shifting, one must try to know the loss, limits, and inherent confusion found in the shift (translating) from Euro-American to African centeredness or from African centered to Euro-American.

As noted earlier, paradigm is a comprehensive model of understanding that establishes viewpoints and rules regarding how one understands reality and identifies problems and how to solve them. In effect, a paradigm identifies what is to be observed and scrutinized. What are the kinds of questions that should be asked and probed for answers in relation to a subject? Which investigation and explorations should be structured or undertaken? How should the results (outcomes) be interpreted? In paradigm shifting, one must simultaneously shift the ontological, cosmological, and axiological appreciations of what constitutes reality—how one knows, and what is to be experienced (ethos, worldview, ideology, and episteme). This required a change in episteme. Episteme determines and influences (1) how reality is defined; (2) the nature of reality; (3) how truth is determined; (4) that which is knowable and can be known; and (5) what the relationship is between knowing (process), the known (subject), and the knower (being). What should or could be done in response to the known? There are several features or assumptions which distinguish an "African" paradigm: (1) the universe is a vital cosmos, (2) the ultimate nature of reality is spirit, (3) human beings are organically related to everything in the universe, (4) knowledge comes from participation with and experience in the universe (reality), and (5) human relatedness is the praxis of our humanity. All humans use their own epistemic reflections, cultural appreciations, and apperceptions about reality to inform how they "know" and "think," which, in turn, allows one to further recognize and record events and experiences as well as make sense out of reality. Hence, the major challenge in shifting episteme,[1] that is, the process of knowing in Black psychology was (is) the need to continually engage in "epistemic reflections" at every stage of the knowing, knowledge production, and praxis (doing) enterprise. From the perspective of the African-centered thought and Black psychology, the shifting from Euro-American psychology to Black psychology has presented the formal challenge of exchanging what is known with rescuing what is unknown. To make this shift, we have had to simultaneously critique the conceptual battery of Euro-American therapeutic ideas while rescuing African-centered language and logic that supported the adoption of concepts and ideas that would inform the new Black psychology healing process. Thus, paradigm shifting and epistemic reflection also reflects the adoption and utilization of "language and logic" that represents and reflects the new thinking, knowing, and ultimately being. In effect, it represents and reflects an epistemic correction or replacement and reclamation where the importance of "languaging" is fundamental. The following requisite correction, clarification, and direction include returning to the source, an African episteme, grand narrative, critical conceptual refinements, praxis of interconnected rings of wellness, and requirements for restoring wellness.

RETURNING TO THE SOURCE

The appreciation and application of personhood, authenticity, and the meaning of Be(ing) require the return to the source of African thought and ideas. The place of returning[2] is ancient Africa or, more specifically, the Nile Valley in Kmt (Egypt). Kmt offers several ideas, impressions, and expressions worthy of interrogation and interpretation in this quest to understand and develop the science of human functioning. The quest flows out of the Nile Valley into the BaNtu expanse and onto the many rivers that cross throughout the African diaspora.

For Kmt, it will be informative to rescue the esoteric and philosophical understanding of African Being through a review of the ideas of genesis, Nu, Skh, the divisions of the soul, and the eight principles of Djehuti. The ancient Kemite/Nubians believed that the Neb-er-tcher evolved from the

primordial substance and facilitated the evolution of forms into phenomena (E. Budge, 1997). The "creative principle" emerged from the
primordial substance; that is, Nu and all phenomena were, in fact, extensions of Nu. The Kemite/Nubians believed in the consubstantiality of all
phenomena. One key to understanding Kemite/Nubian philosophy can
be found in the belief about the meaning of the person. Because the person was a manifestation or expression of Nu, the primordial substance,
the ancients regarded the "form" of the human being as destined to live
forever. Hence, institutions were developed to enable the person to evolve
in response to the challenges of nature. The human person, like other
forms, has an unchanging value and evolves in response to the demands
of that value. The ancients regarded the primordial substance, Nu, as
infinite. The infinity operated in terms of its law, which was its will. As a
manifestation of Nu, the person represents a manifestation of "the Law."
Ancient African genesis is best understood by noting that the nature,
character, and quality of the defining spirit or energy was expressed as a
deity which served as the generating idea. Ancient African genesis can be
rescued at the places named or called Ineb Hedj (Memphis), Iuni
(Heliopolis), Un/Khmunu (Hermopholis), and Waset (Thebes). The place
named Ineb Hedj (the White Wall) was the major deity was Ptah. Ineb
Hedji was founded around 3100 BCE by Menes of Tanis, who united the
two kingdoms of Kemet; with some 30,000 inhabitants, it was by far the
largest settlement worldwide at the time. The name *Memphis* is
the Greek deformation of the Egyptian name of Pepi I's (VIth dynasty)
pyramid, *Men-nefer*. Memphis reached a peak of prestige under the 6th
Dynasty as a center of the cult of Ptah. At Ineb Hedj (Memphis), the
creative principle was "unification"—the place named Iuni (Heliopolis).
The major deity was Atum. Iuni was occupied since the Predynastic
Period. The Pyramid Texts of Dynasty V and VI state that "Out of Nun
rose the creator of the world Atum" or the Primeval Mound, "lord to the
limit of the sky" and "lord of Heliopolis," who self-developed into a
being, standing on a raised mound—the primeval mound—which
became the Benben, a pyramid-shaped stone, regarded as the dwelling
place of the sun god. The chief deity of Heliopolis was the god Atum,
who was worshipped in the primary temple, which was known by the
names *Per-Aat* (*pr-at*; "Great House") and *Per-Atum* (*pr-tmw*; "House of
Atum"). The city was also the original source of the worship of the
Ennead pantheon. At Iunu (Heliopolis), the Creative Principle was Self-
Generation. The place named (Un) Khmunu was called "the City of the
Eight" (Hermopholis). At Un, the major Deities were Tehuti (Ogdoad,
Aten), and the male and female aspects of reality were imagined as the
four creative powers or sources: NUN and NAUNET represented the
primeval waters, HEH and HAUHET represented eternity, KUK
and KUAKET represented darkness, and AMUN and AMAUNET

represented air (or that which is hidden). The Creative Principle was Balance. The place was named Waset. In the place of Waset (Thebes), the major deity was Amun (Mut, Khons, Montu, Buchis, Sobek). At Waset, the deity Amun was thought to transcend creation and was elevated to become the primeval creator god, being above, before, and beyond creation. Amun was "he who fashioned himself," before anything else came into existence. At Waset, the Creative Principle was Being/Becoming. The ancient Kemetic imagination conceived of exoteric instruction as the training of the sense and the mind by applying the "Laws of MAAT" (truth, justice, righteousness). The goal was to bring about understanding of the conformity of the name of each thing with its true nature, the appearance given to manufactured things (i.e., shape, color decoration) with their purpose and function, and a building's measurement and proportions with the laws it was meant to teach. The Esoteric Instruction: *Symbolic and Subliminal* (esoteric) instruction was designed to train the senses and mind to interpret the signs and symbols in reality by understanding the lessons of Tehuti and Seshat, god and goddess of mathematics, measurement, magic, and writing and the neter of writing, geometrical patterns, and shapes occurring in nature.

Kemetic (Ancient African)		
Esoteric and Philosophical Imagination		
Place	Deity	Generative Idea
Ineb Hadj (Memphis)	Ptah	Unification
Iunu (Heliopolis)	Atum	Self-Generation
Un/Khmunu (Hermopholis)	Tehuti	Balance
Waset (Thebes)	Amun	Being/Becoming

The primordial substance (Nu) defined, proclaimed, evolved, and expressed itself as "Human" in order to discover more satisfying dimensions of being. Nu was pictured as a woman portrayed as a star-filled sky, arched over the earth with her fingers and toes touching the four cardinal points or directions of north, south, east, and west—the goddess (Nu or Nut) of the sky and all heavenly bodies.

The Ancient African (Kemetic) imagination concerning the expression (division) of spirit is equally informative. The psychic, or spiritual constitution or, more accurately, the expression of the spirit in Ancient Egyptian thought, was believed to comprise seven parts. The Ka, or principle body, was the first division of the psychic nature. The essence of all the divisions of the soul was the Ka of God. Upon physical death (transition), disintegration returns to the elements from which it came. The Ba (soul of breath) was the second division of the psychic nature. The Ba was the invisible source of all visible functions and represented the essence of all things. It represented the transmission of the breath of life. The Ancient Kemites believed that there was only one power, symbolically represented as "the breath." It was transmitted from the ancestors to the descendants. This power or energy has always existed and will always exist. The third division of the psychic nature was called the Khaba (the veil or cover). It is the luminous intangible covering of the vital principle, Ba. It governs human emotion and motion. It is thought to be responsible for sustaining the sensory perceptions and the phenomena of color, total harmony, and the circulation of blood. It was the abode of the psychic pattern by which the body was afflicted. It was believed to play a significant part in disease and responsible for delusions. The fourth division of the psychic nature was called Akhu, known as the seat of intelligence and mental perception. In the area of Akhu, the whole mystery of the human mind is to be comprehended. The Akhu was characterized by attributes like judgment, analysis, and mental reflection, which could be trained and disciplined, so as to be dedicated to the service of the higher being. The concerns of the Akhu were primarily the survival of its own thinking processes. The fifth division of the psychic nature was the Seb or ancestral soul. It does not manifest itself in humans until puberty or adolescence. It represents and signifies the power of the human being to generate its own kind. The Seb is in effect the self-creative power of Being. The sixth division of the psychic nature, called Putah, represented the "first intellectual father." Associated with the mental maturity of the individual, the coming of Putah marked the union of the brain with the mind. It was the Putah that established the fact of the person and from the moment of its manifestation or attainment it was believed that intellect (i.e., will and intent) alone governs conduct. The final division of the soul was the Atmu.

Considered the divine or the eternal soul, the seventh creation inspired the breath of life everlasting. In ritual, this division of the soul is represented as parenthood that symbolically stood for the presence of full creative powers and perpetual continuation. Although Atmu represented the presence of such fullness, enwrapping and serving as the essence of all the divisions of the soul was the Ka of God. In some texts, the Ka is thought of as the sum of the above-mentioned seven. However, this is only true if the sum is considered greater than the total of its parts. The Ka was the divine spirit that endowed all things, and which survived past the physical life of the individual. The Ka was thought to have magical powers and could cause the dead to live again in the thoughts of the survivors and could even enter into a mummified being, animate it internally, and cause it to have a continued inner life or existence. The Ka was the intangible likeness of the living. It appeared in the dream state and some believed that it actually traveled independently of the body during those times.

Classical African (Scholarship) episteme is found in what was misappropriated as "Hermes Trismegistus" (300 BCE), given the title of "Three times Great Great," and sometimes called Thot, Thoth—Hermes. The eight principles of Djehuti (c. 6000–3150 BCE), God of knowledge, Medu Netcher, and wisdom, Maintainer of the Universe were (1) Mentalism—All is mind and the universe is Mental; (2) Correspondence—As Above, So Below, as Below so Above; (3) Vibration—Nothing rests, everything moves, everything vibrates; (4) Polarity—Like and unlike are the same, opposites are identical in nature but different in degree, and extremes meet. All truths are but half-truths; (5) Rhythm—Everything flows out and in, everything has its tides, all things rise and fall, and the pendulum swing manifests in everything . . . rhythm compensates; (6) Cause and Effect—Every cause has an effect, every effect has a cause, everything happens according to law. Chance is but a name for a law not recognized . . . nothing escapes the law; (7) Gender—Gender is in everything, everything has its masculine and feminine principle; (8) Complementarity—Being is dual and needs other to enhance or improve, to be complete, make whole.

Ancient Kemetic Black/African foundations [of the] universe[3] origins inform us that "primordial substance existed prior to Neb-er-tcher evolved and facilitated evolutions of forms into phenomena." Ancient Egyptian thinkers posited existence of states of matter before God and all his creations. Better still, God as creator himself emerged from this primal matter, itself uncreated. Ancient Egyptians posited uncreated reality (that which was neither born nor made); substratum without form or shape, an amorphous reality, named "Nwn" (Nobles, 1997, p. 39) before god the demiurge. Demiurge a being (other than The Supreme Being) is credited with the creation of the world.[4]

Theophile Obenga (1992), with expertise in Ancient Egyptian philosophy and Egyptian thought systems, advances that these philosophies laid foundations and erected scaffoldings for temple architecture. They were the decisive organizational influence on construction of pyramids. They provided philosophical foundations for understanding origins of the universe predating contemporary thinking. Egyptian thought systems imposed an almost abstract precision on the performance of essential rites and were, without a doubt, a philosophy of the uncreated, conscious of itself, making the pharaonic system a dynamic system, in the potent, complete sense of the term (p. 41). It was upon this concept of the "uncreated" an eminently philosophical concept that the ancient Egyptians organized their worldview.[5]

Key to understanding ancient Kemetic philosophy as worldview is found in Kemetic beliefs about the meaning of the person. Because the person was seen as a manifestation or expression of Nu, primordial substance, the ancients regarded the "form" of human beings as destined to live forever. Hence, institutions were developed to enable the person to evolve in response to the challenges of nature.[6] In classical African Kemetic philosophy, the significance of the human being is found in the fact of "Being, Becoming, and Belonging." Divine law governed human beings and human reality and the basic divine law was simply "To Be" and in being, one was the "creative cause" which made humans divine. Divine law was, in turn, translated into an enduring moral mandate, which stated that "To Be" was permanently guaranteed by the human instinct "To Become." The moral mandate of African humanity was "to become and in becoming," humans revealed their "belongingness" to God(-liness), that is, capacity to be the creative cause.

African and Black/African-centered scholars have inferred and interpreted contemporary representations of African cosmological "creative principles." Kemetic personhood is revealed in the symbolism of MAAT and pharaoh's spirituality because MAAT is believed to be the proper quality of all Being and Becoming. MAAT principles rule cosmic, metaphysical, and physical planes of reality. In its cosmic (spiritual) expression, MAAT represents harmony, order, stability (unchanging), and security (eternal). In its metaphysical expression, MAAT represents uprightness, righteousness, truth, and justice. As the metaphysical meaning of being, MAAT reveals that beingness (personhood or character) is based on the belief that a just and proper relationship characterizes everything, including the relationship of the rulers and the ruled, the victors and the vanquished, directors and the directed, and the teachers and the taught; and that something is true not only because it is susceptible to testing and validation but because its beingness is recognized as being in its true and proper place in a divinely ruled universe. In its physical expression, MAAT represents levelness, evenness, straightness, correctness, regularity, and balance. As cosmic law, MAAT reveals that beingness (personhood or character) is the fact that "the order of all things, physical and spiritual, whether created or manifested should be established at the beginning (of becoming) and remain for all time (throughout Beingness)."

In Kemetic beliefs, the individual is a manifestation or expression of Nu, the primordial substance . . . a special being who is both subject and greater than subject defined by uniqueness, relatedness, connection, and coherence—all of which are bounded and defined by a common collective spirit. The Kemites believed that spirit was the energy, force, or power that is both the inner essence and the outer envelope of human beingness. As energy, spirit or spiritness (the condition of being a spirit) thus served to ignite and enliven the human state of being. Moreover, human beings believed to experience this spiritness simultaneously as both a metaphysical state and an ethereal extension or connection into and between the supra world of Egyptian deities and the interworld of other beings, and the inner world of the self.

Going from North Africa to South Africa, we can see evidence of the common African meaning of the person as spirit.

AFRICAN EPISTEME

The call for asserting an African episteme is, in part, rooted in the fact that the Western Grand Narrative has supported a mindset that is grounded in ideations that privilege difference, aristocracy, elitism, classism, racism, sexism, genetic inferiority, and caste attribution, resulting in a "grand narrative" that, in fact, reflects deep intrinsic Western beliefs (both descriptive and explanatory discourse) as universal. What is essential to the Western Grand Narrative is the idea of a "linear hierarchical oppositional structure" that is the implicit legacy of the Western mindset. Falsely accepted as universal, the idea of a linear hierarchical oppositional structure is the core problematic issue in the quest to define, describe, and explain African notions of human functioning. Though seldom recognized as particular and even equivalent conceptions of reality, the African ways of knowing are different from those found in the Western world. African reality is often described as being made up of three interrelated (not oppositional) hierarchical worlds consisting of the immediate perceptible world (the microcosmos); the intermediate world of spirits, genies, and beneficial and malevolent forces (the mesocosmos); and the world beyond the senses, the realm of the Divine, ancestors, and Spirit Beings (the macrocosmos) (Sow, 1980, p. 48). In the African structure, it is believed that there is constant, perpetual, perceivable, and continuous relationship between those who dwell in the multiple realms of reality (humans, spirits, and the Divine). Hence, an African episteme must include considerations and comprehension relative to all three realms. With the centrality or essentiality of spirit, the African process of knowing and comprehension may be better understood as the interplay of radiations, vibrations, fields, planes, waves, and points of energy between and among the realms of reality. In *Seeking the Sakhu,* I (Nobles, 2006, pp. 349–350) suggest that spirit or spiritness is the belief that the complexity of being a person (as immaterial and material) gives one an intrinsic human value and that the person is, in fact, a process characterized by the divinely governed laws of essence, appearing, perfecting, and compassion. The concept of "spirit" or "essence" as defined by African thought further suggests that the examination of African American psychology should be guided by strategies of knowing that allow for the examination of the continuation and refinement, across time, space, and place, of the African conceptualization of human beingness. In this regard, I (Nobles, 2015, pp. 407–409) have offered a radical refinement of the African conception of reality wherein I posit that all is spirit or energy with different expressions and experiences. Those beings and entities that dwell in the microcosmos, mesocosmos, and macrocosmos are all spirit defined and spirit driven. Accordingly, it is believed that African people experience spirit or spiritness (Grills, 2002, pp. 10–24; Nobles, 1997, pp. 203–213) simultaneously as a metaphysical state and an ethereal extension or connection into and between the supra world of the Deities, the interworld of other beings, and the inner world of oneself. As such, as intellectual mindset the African epistemic reflection would posit that real(ity) is spirit made manifest, which, in turn, would allow for the framing of the process of knowing with constructs like commonality, centeredness, transformation, transcendence, improvisation, inspiration, agency, will, revelation, invocation, intention, and the "power of the word." Hence, rather than posit an "ambivalent, oppositional" dialectic, African-centered theorists and practitioners should consider the differing and special relationship between and among the various expressions of spirit within and between the realms of reality. By adopting African-centered epistemic reflections, cultural appreciations, and apperceptions about reality, our knowing framework and intellectual mindset would allow for further recognition and recordings that make better sense of African events and experiences. It is the understanding of the fullness or completeness of African being, becoming, and belonging, ergo, Africanness that is central to the understanding of indigenous knowledge systems as praxis.

AFRICAN GRAND NARRATIVE

An African Grand Narrative is reflected in the voice of people of African ancestry, which is seldom and often ignored or not heard. Growing out of African people's cultural grounding, meanings of being human, and historical relations, an African voice reflects the subjective and collective ability to express the essential and authentic experience of life and living for African people. In contrast to the Western Grand Narrative, an African Grand Narrative as *Kmt-Nubian/BaNtu-Kongo* understands that all in reality is Spirit or Energy and that a particular process of knowing emerges from African genesis or creation myths, the meaning of being human, and the concept of life and death. The Kmt-Nubian/BaNtu-Kongo (African) Grand Narrative privileges the sense of personhood, synergy, circularity, interconnectedness, wholism, and collectivism. The *Kmt-Nubian/Bantu Grand Narrative* reflects a particular intellectual mindset that posits real(ity) based on and in Spiritness (see Nobles, 2015). An African Grand Narrative would and should reflect and represent the voice of African people on the continent and throughout the diaspora. Accordingly, I propose that we formulate an African Grand Narrative based in Kmt-Nubia/BaNtu-Kongo thought that interrogates the knowing implications of the classical civilizations of Kmt (Egypt) and Nubia, and the ancient beliefs of the BaNtu and Kongo people. Such an African Grand Narrative would posit that reality is Spirit and that a particular process of knowing emerges from African genesis or creation myths, meaning of being human, and concept of life and death. Parenthetically, it is important to provide a clarification of this idea of Spiritness as distinct from spirituality. I have suggested that Spiritness pertains to the condition of *being spirit* as distinct from spirituality, which pertains to having the quality of being spiritual. It is believed that African people experience their spiritness (Grills, 2002; Nobles, 1997) simultaneously as a metaphysical state and an ethereal extension or connection into and between the *supra* world of the Deities, the *inter*-world of other beings, and the *inner* world of oneself. Spiritness is often misconceived as spirituality and deemed a religious quality. It is more akin to physics than religion—the sense of personhood, synergy, inter-connectedness, circularity, wholism, and collectivism. Grounded in African epistemological reflections, the African Grand Narrative would privilege a particular intellectual mindset that would posit that real(ity) is based on Spiritness, as defined above. The idea of Spiritness, in turn, would allow for the framing of the process of knowing with constructs like commonality, centeredness, transformation, transcendence, improvi-sation, and inspiration.

CRITICAL CONCEPTUAL REFINEMENTS

Given an African episteme, the following two conceptual shifts are essential: (1) personhood and (2) authenticity. Unlike the Western para-digm, knowing, life, and living for the African is never experienced "individually" as an agent that is separate and distinct from all other "individuals." Until imposed by the West, there was no such thing as an individual. The guiding principle for African people has been and remains the retention of a communal ethos that emphasizes the impor-tance of the collective. (Be)ing is represented as within the existence of the family or tribe and experienced as "personhood." What is misper-ceived and misunderstood as the individual is, in fact, personage or personhood as the special (and possibly unique) personal attributes, characteristics, and qualities of a particular manifestation of the com-munal or community (whole). In the language of the BaNtu, being a human being is to be a *ala ba muntu*—a person is a known, knowing, and knowable spirit. Therefore, personhood theory is the study of the journey (development) of the known, knowing, and knowable human spirit. Accordingly, it was noted (see Nobles, 2006, p. 1), that (1) a person, by law, is human; (2) a person is spirit manifest; (3) a person has to *evolve* over the distance of being human; (4) human com-passion dictates that a person cannot be thrown away; (5) a person is defined by uniqueness, relatedness, connection, and coherence; (6) a *person is a person because there are other people;* (7) a person is human because of an indisputable connection between the person and God (belonging); (8) a person is able to say what and who one is and to define oneself as valuable (being); and (9) to become human is the only important task of the person (becoming). Thus, to be human is to *belong* to Divine energy, to *be* inherently valued and valuable, and to be *becoming* perfectible. The overall aim of personhood is to teach everyone the "essentiality" of the community for one's own survival and ascension and the formation of one's identity as a person. We speak of *personhood* instead of personality to suggest the fullness of one's human expression that evolves over the arc of one's life. Thus, the whole of life is a process of learning to attain personhood and become fully human. J. K. Ngubane (1979) suggests the African understanding of the person is as "a 'protein' evaluation of being human; [it] that flowed into Nile Valley ['s] high culture of the Ancient Kemites and subsequently created clusters of similar conceptions all over Africa" (p. 62). What is recognized as African culture and civilization is the combined social conventions and inventions emerging from a common African meaning of the person.

The second essential shift concerns the idea of authenticity. Authenticity is larger than mere identity development, as we commonly think of it. Authenticity means that one's identity is grounded in a collective ethnic and cultural consciousness. The clear identification of African ideals, images, and interests as codified in African worldviews and ideologies provides the only clear and consistent template for understanding African reality. A people's worldview is their most comprehensive idea about order and understanding and beliefs about the nature of reality and the meaning of being, the proper role of society, and the way things are or should be. World view is fundamental and comes from ancestral insight (inspiration), historical experience, and psychocultural retentions and inventions. The African worldview can be and has been influenced or distorted. Regarding both the continental and diasporan African worldview, distortions and alien impositions have occurred.[7] African worldviews change via political domination; cultural exploitation or appropriation; and strategies of unsophisticated falsification of facts, information, or ideas beliefs; integrated modification to distort, suppress or modify facts, information, and ideas, and scientific colonialism wherein facts, information, ideas beliefs are conceptual, incarcerated, locked up with erroneous or alien concepts. For African ascendant people, the resultant impact is that our self-interest choices and chances are driven by a persistent, abnormal, and irrational fear or avoidance of things African, that is, Afrophobia; a positive unwarranted positive feeling of love, liking, and affection for European things, Europhilia; and a violent derangement of the mind due to Greco-Roman thought and ideas, Grecomnia.

Nevertheless, the cultural worldview (resources) of a community are the bases for both personal and collective identity. Authenticity best captures the intent of articulating a theory of human beingness that is centered in African realities. As noted, through an African lens, episteme (knowing/understanding) concerns itself with (1) how reality is defined; (2) what the nature of reality is; (3) how truth is determined; (4) what is KNOWABLE—can be known; and (5) what the relationship between KNOWING (process), the KNOWN (subject), and the KNOWER (being) is—what should or could be done in response to the known. The idea of authenticity allows for the framing of the process of knowing with constructs like commonality, centeredness, transformation, transcend-ence, improvisation, inspiration, agency, will, revelation, invocation, intention, and the "power of the word."

Accordingly, personhood and authenticity require the rescue of the mean-ing of Be(ing), which is to be spirit/energy in a reality of spirit/energy. From African deep thought and wisdom, we are Spirit Beings and not human beings. The *experience* of Be(ing) human, the *expression* of Be(ing) human, and the *essence* of Be(ing) human itself is all spirit. As Spirit Be(ings), we are trifold, unfolding, vibrating, radiating energy/spirit (experience) of yet-to-live, living, and after-living spirit likened to a living sun, possessing a "known, knowing and knowable" spirit (energy or power) through which one has an enduring relationship with the total perceptible and ponderable multiuniverse.

> *We are spirit beings housed in a physical container having a human experience.*

As *yet-to-live spirit/energy,* Be(ing) is the molecular concentration of potential and possibility.

As *living spirit/energy,* Be(ing) is concentrated essence, in material form, manifested for a particular purpose. As *after-living spirit/energy,* Be(ing) is the invisible expression of the essence of spirit/energy vibrating and radiating at different unseeable energy levels (fields) as the Ancestors, living–dead, dwellers-of-heaven, Orisa, Lwa, or all those in the invisible realm. *We are the Ancestors.* All that exists are, therefore, different con-crete expressions of Spirit (Ntu).

PERSONHOOD IN AFRICA

Kemetic beliefs about the person are well documented and upon review, one can see that the Kemetic meaning of the person is similar to the meaning of the person reflected throughout the major cultures of Africa. In *The Book of Knowing the Evolutions of Ra* (Atem, 2006), the creator God, Neb-er-tcher, states

> I am he who evolved himself under the form of the God Khepera. I, the evolver of the evolutions, evolved myself, after many evolutions and developments which came forth from my mouth. No heavens existed, and no earth, and no terrestrial animals or reptiles had come into being. I formed them out of the inert mass of watery matter worked, I found no place whereupon to stand. I was alone. There existed none other with me. I laid the foundations of all things by my will, and all things evolved themselves therefrom. I sent forth Shu and Tefnut out from myself. Shu

and Tefnut gave birth to Nut and Seb, and Nut gave birth to Osiris, Horus-Khent-an-maa, Sut, Isis and Nephtys. At one birth, one after the other, and their many children multiply upon this earth.

These Ancient Africans believed that the Neb-er-tcher evolved himself from the primordial substance and facilitated the evolution of forms into phenomena. The creative principle emerged out of the primordial substance; that is, Nu and all phenomena were, in fact, extensions of Nu. The Kemites believed in the consubstantiality of all phenomena. The ancient Kemetic definition of the *human being* (Nobles, 1986b) emphasized, at minimum, the consubstantiality of the primordial substance (and phenomenal expressions); the primacy of the person; perpetual evolution (perfectibility); and eternal life. The character of the person was continually challenged in response to the challenge of one's destiny. For the Kemites, the challenge was, through perfecting, to live throughout the millennia, to be forever "noble," to be "the princes of eternity."

Like the Kemites, the KiZulu-speaking people of South Africa believed that all phenomena (*Uluthu*) had their origins in a "living consciousness (Ngubane, 1976)," which they called *UQOBU*. The person evolved from the *UQOBU* in response to *Umthetho weMvelo* (the law of appearing); the demands of *Isimu* (one's nature) and *Ukuma Njalu* (perpetual evolution). The person, according to the Zulu, is a self-defining value and that life's purpose for the person is perpetual evolution. The Zulu's ideal emphasized the primacy of the person and the creation of a society that equipped, enabled, and ensured that the person would realize the promise of being or becoming human (1976, p. 77) (*Ukuba Ngumuntu*). As a person, the components of realizing the promise of being human are (a) the person by law is human (*Umuntu Ngumuntu*), (b) the person has to evolve over the distance of being human (*Amabanga Okuba Ngumuntu*), and (c) human compassion dictates that the person cannot be "thrown" away (1976, p. 93) (*Ukuba Ngumuntu*). Like almost all African people, the BaZulu have an ancient text, the *Izaga*, in which they define the meaning of what it is to be a person (J. K. Ngubane, 1979, p. 60). The text of wise sayings contains the Zulu interpretations of the teachings of the Sudic philosophy. Within these teachings, the Zulu say *Umuntu Ngumuntu*, meaning, "the person is human." In this same regard, Dr. Marimba Ani (1994) teaches that the BaNtu belief about the concept of the person is crystallized in the saying, *Umuntu Ngu Muntu Nga BaNtu*, which means "A person is a person because there are people." In believing that the primordial substance was infinite, the Zulu believe that all phenomena were made of the primordial substance. The person was one such phenomenon. The ancient Zulu philosophers taught in this regard that, through the *Umuntu Ngumuntu*, the human person was unique in that the person defined oneself and is essentially knowledgeable of one's own intrinsic value. For the Zulu to be human is to be able to say what and who one is and to be able to define oneself as a value.

Moving into West Africa, we find the Akan, who consider a human being to be composed of three elements. The first element is the *Okra,* which constitutes the innermost self, the essence of the person (Gyekye, 1997, p. 9). The *Okra* is considered the living soul of the person and is sometimes referred to as the *Okrateasafo.* As the living soul, the *Okra* is identical with life. It is also the embodiment and transmitter of the individual's *Nkrabea* (destiny). As the life force, the *Okra* is linked to *Honhom* (breath) (1997, p. 95). The *Honam,* however, is the tangible and recognizable manifestation of the presence of the *Okra.* The second element of the person is the *Sunsum.* The term *Sunsum* is used to refer to all unperceivable, mystical beings and forces. It is the activating principle in the person (1997, p. 88). The *Sunsum* is what molds the child's personality and disposition. It is that which determines the character. The *Okra,* in turn, manifests itself in the world of experience through the *Sunsum.* The final component is simply the *Honam* (the body), which is made up of *Ntoro* and *Mogya.* While the *Okra* and the *Sunsum* come from *Onyame* (God), the *Ntoro* and the *Mogya* are derived from other humans, one's parents. In their conception of the nature of the person, the Akan believe that the *Ntoro* is derived from the father's sperm and the *Mogya* is derived from the mother's blood. The *Okra* and the *Sunsum* constitute a spiritual unity. Hence, the person is made up of two principal components, the immaterial/spiritual (*Okra and Sunsum*) and the material/physical (*Honam*). In terms of the relation between the soul and the body, Akan thinkers contend that not only does the body influence the soul, but the soul also influences the body. The Akan believe that the relation between the soul (*Okra and Sunsum*) and the body (*Honam*) is so close that they comprise an indissoluble and indivisible unity. Hence, the person is a homogeneous entity or value.

The Yoruba people believe that the person is made up of a spirit and a body (Opoku, 1978, p. 92). The body or *Ara* is formed by the divinity, *Orisha-nla.* It is through the *Ara* that man responds to his environment. It is the part of the person which can be touched and felt. It can be damaged and disintegrated after death. The spirit component of the person is the *Emi* (spirit). The *Emi* gives life to the person. The *Emi* is the divine element of the person and links the person directly to God. Upon the death of the person, the *Emi* returns to *Elemi* (the owner of the spirit, God) and continues to live. As a person, one also possesses an inner head or *Ori Inu.* The *Ori Inu* is given directly by *Olodumare.* It is the person's personal spirit. The *Ori Inu* is the guardian of the self and the carrier of one's destiny. It also influences the personality of the person. In addition to the *Emi* and the *Ori Inu,* the person has an *Okan* (p. 93). The word *Okan* means heart, but as a constituent component of the person, it represents the immaterial element that is the seat of intelligence, thought, and action. Hence, it is sometimes referred to as the "heart–soul" of the person. The *Okan* is believed to exist even before the person's birth. It is the *Okan* of the ancestors that is reincarnated in the newborn child. To be a person, the Yoruba also believe that one must have *Ori* and *Eje*. The *Ori* rules, controls, and guides the person's life and actually activates the person. The *Ori* is the bearer of one's destiny and helps the person to fulfill what they came to earth to do. The *Ori* is simultaneously the "essence of the person" and the person's "guardian and protector" (p. 93). The *Ori* is closely associated with the *Emi*. The *Eje* is the blood. It is the physical expression of an electrochemical/magnetic energy that is the force that binds and animates life. The Yoruba also believe that the *Iye* is a component of the person. The *Iye* is the immaterial element that is sometimes referred to as the mind (p. 93). The person also has *Ojiji* (shadow). The *Ojiji* is a constant companion throughout one's life and ceases to exist when the *Ara* (body) dies.

According to the Mende, the person is made up of the *Ngafa* (the spirit) and the *Nduwai* (the flesh) (Opoku, 1978, p. 94). The *Ngafa* is immaterial and is provided by the mother. It leaves the body at death and goes into the land of the spirits. The *Ngafa* is the psychic constituent of the person. The *Nduwai* is the physical part of the person and is provided by the father. The *Nduwai* is, in part, contained in the seminal fluid. The shadow (*Nenei*) is also part of the person (Harris & Sawyer, 1968, p. 88) and is believed to report the death of the body to God. The Mende believe that a healthy spirit (*Ngatha*) produces a state of *Guhun* (total well-being). The person's name is closely associated with his *Ngaf*. The significance of the name is that the Mende believe that a person's *Ngafa* can travel from the person during sleep or other state of unconsciousness. However, a person can be revived or awakened when one's name is called repeatedly. The Mende, therefore, believe that the person's name may be the component that wakes up the *Ngafa* or the human spirit.

In their discussion of African elements of human beingness, Grills and Rowe (1996) note that the Lebou people of Senegal believe that the person is, first and foremost, comprised of the *Fit* (vital energy or life force), which is what makes them human. *Fit* is referred to as the spiritual heart of the person. The part of the person that gives one physical life is called *Roo*. This is the breath of life which leaves the body at death. The Lebou believe that each of us has a spiritual shadow that is always present and protects the person. This shadow is called the *Takondeer*. Additionally, to be a person, one must possess and cultivate the qualities of *Yel* (intelligence) and *Sago* (reason). Finally, to be a person is to have a *Raab*. *Raabs* are constellations of spiritual forces, like the Yoruba Orishas, that possess, guide, and protect the person. They are, in fact, ancestral spirits that influence and shape the personality and behavior of the person.

THE BANTU

The BaNtu are especially important because not only do they represent almost three-fourths of the African cultural-linguistic heritage, they in the so-called BaNtu expansion also represent the unrecognized bridge between classical and historical African beliefs and contemporary continental and diasporan epistemic legacy and cultural retentions. The so-called BaNtu expansion first originated around the Benue-Cross rivers area in Southeastern Nigeria and spread over Africa to the Zambia area. Sometime in the second millennium BCE, the BaNtu were forced to expand into the rainforest of Central Africa. Later, the BaNtu began a more rapid second phase of expansion beyond the forests into Southern and Eastern Africa reaching modern-day Zimbabwe and South Africa. Another theory held that the BaNtu originated from the Congo and spread out to the north, east, and south. Whether going from north to south or south to north it should be clear that the BaNtu spread out over most of Africa and with the experience of the slave trade spread equally throughout the new world. The primary evidence for this great expansion (Ehret, 2001), one of the largest in human history, has been linguistic, namely that the languages spoken in sub-Equatorial Africa are remarkably similar to each other, to the degree that it is unlikely that they began diverging from each other more than 3,000 years ago. The BaNtu people with their culture, language, family, spiritual beliefs, and philosophical ideas are the very people stolen and kidnapped in the Transatlantic slave trade. In effect, BaNtu beliefs and ideas were embedded in the various peoples who were stolen and kidnapped.

Africans on the continent and throughout the diaspora are fundamentally BaNtu people. In fact, it is only in understanding the BaNtu-Kongo ideas and meanings of being human that one will be able to better or more fully determine the impact of the Trans-Saharan and Transatlantic slave trade. The BaNtu-Kongo believe that the heated force of kalunga blew up and down as a huge storm of projectiles, *kimbwandende*, fusing together a huge mass. In the process of cooling, solidification of the fused mass occurred, giving birth to the earth (Fu-Kiau, 2001). In effect, the BaNtu believe that all of reality (*kalunga*) is fundamentally a process of perpetual and mutual sending and receiving of Spirit (energy) in the form of waves and radiations. *Kalunga* or reality is the totality, the completeness of all life. It is an ocean of energy, a force in motion. *Kalunga* is everything, sharing life and becoming life continually after life itself. As the totality or the complete living, *kalunga* comprises both a visible realm (*ku nseke*) and an invisible realm (*ku mpemba*). The visible physical world has Spirit (energy) as its most important element or nature. Referred to as *nkisi* (medicine), the spirit element of the physical (visible) world has the power to care, cure, heal, and guide. The invisible (spiritual) world (*ku mpemba*) is composed of human experience, ancestor experience, and the soul–mind experience. The *ku mpemba* has Spirit (energy) as its most important element or nature. In effect, if reality (visible and invisible) is, it is Spirit. All that exists are, therefore, different concrete expressions of Spirit. In effect, Being is being Spirit in a reality of spirit. Fu-Kiau (2001) further clarifies that the human being or *muntu* is a "threefold unfolding" experience in the realms of yet-to-live, living, and after-living. He further notes that a human being is a living sun (energy), possessing "knowing and knowable" spirit (energy) through which spirit in human form has an enduring relationship with the total perceptible and ponderable universe. The BaNtu-Kongo believe that diverse forces and waves of energy govern life and surround humans. This fire-force called *kalunga* is complete in and of itself and emerges within the emptiness or nothingness and becomes the source of life on earth.

In BaNtu thought, *what is* real(ity) is called *kalunga,* which is fundamentally a process of perpetual and mutual sending and receiving of Spirit (energy) in the form of waves and radiations. The material universe is only the perception of real(ity), that is, in fact, nonlocalized, immutable, and eternal spirit. The totality or the complete living that is real(ity) (*Kalunga*) is composed of both a visible realm (*Ku Nseke, Aye*) and an invisible realm (*Ku Mpemba, Orun*). The visible realm is considered the microcosmos, the immediate perceptible world. The invisible realm is considered the mesocosmos, the intermediate world of spirits, genies, and beneficial and malevolent forces. The macrocosmos, the world beyond the senses, is the realm of the Divine, Ancestors, and Spirit beings. Reality consists of the visible and the invisible with the invisible being far greater than the visible. Though seldom recognized as a particular and even equivalent conception of reality, the African ways of knowing are different from those found in the Western world. African reality is often described as being made up of three interrelated (not oppositional) hierarchical worlds consisting of the immediate perceptible world (the microcosmos); the intermediate world of spirits, genies, and beneficial and malevolent forces (the mesocosmos); and the world beyond the senses, the realm of the Divine, ancestors, and spirit beings (the macrocosmos) (Sow, 1980, p. 48). In the African structure, it is believed that there are constant, perpetual, perceivable, and continuous relationships between those who dwell in the multiple realms of reality (humans, spirits, and the Divine).

According to Ngubane (1976, p. 77) the central teachings of the BaNtu is that all things originated from *UQOBU* and evolve in response to the challenge of their nature. In discussing BaNtu philosophy, Kagame (1989) notes that all that exists can be subsumed under one of four categories of *Ntu* or Spirit. *Ntu*, in this regard, is thought to be the universal expression of force or Spirit. *Ntu*, inseparable from Umu, is Being itself.

It is the cosmic universal force. *UbuNtu* is Spirit in which Being and beings coalesce. The underlying logic of *UbuNtu* and African language and logic is exemplary of African deep thought and philosophy. In terms of *UbuNtu*, the construct *Ntu* is thought to be the universal expression of force or spirit. *Ntu*, inseparable from *Umu*, is Being itself (Kagame, 1989). *UbuNtu* is, therefore, spirit in which Being and beings coalesce. It is the cosmic universal force. Conceptually, *Ntu*, as a modal point at which being assumes concrete form, is reflected in four categories of expression in BaNtu philosophy. In effect, there is one essence with four categories of expression. Human beings (*Mu Ntu* or Muntu) are expressions of spirit or force (*Ntu*). Place and Time (*Ha Ntu* or Hantu) are equally expressions of spirit or force (*Ntu*). All the material objects (*Ki Ntu* or Kintu) like mountains, other animals, rivers, and so on are spirit expressions (*Ntu*). Joy, beauty, laughter, love, emotions, and so on (*Ku Ntu* or Kuntu) are equally spirit expressions (*Ntu*). This notion of spirit or force or power makes no distinction between spirit and matter. Matter is not in the BaNtu conceptualization a manifestation of spirit. Matter and spirit are not separate. They are not different or apart. Reality is not a duality of matter and spirit. *UbuNtu* is all that is or "be." Conceptually, *Ntu*, as a modal point at which being assumes concrete form, is reflected in four categories of expression in BaNtu philosophy. In effect, there is one essence with four categories of expression. The categories are *Mu Ntu, Ki Ntu, Ha Ntu*, and *Ku Ntu*. All beings, all expressions of spirit can *Mu Ntu or Muntu; Ha Ntu or Hantu Ki Ntu or Kintu Ku Ntu or Kuntu*. Human beings are spirit (energy)—Knowing and Knowable spirit, including the dwellers of the afterlife (dead), those yet-to-be-born as well as the angels, orishas, loas, and ancestors. Place and time are spirit (energy)—Activated by *Mu Ntu* material objects are spirit (energy)—Activated by *Mu Ntu* Emotions and feelings are spirit (energy)—Activated by *Mu Ntu* be found within one of these categories. All that exists will express itself as one of these expressions. Human beings (*Mu Ntu or Muntu*) are an expression of spirit or force. Place and Time (*Ha Ntu or Hantu*) are equally expressions of spirit or force. All the material objects (*Ki Ntu or Kintu*) like mountains, other animals, rivers, and so on are spirit expressions. Joy, beauty, laughter, love, emotions, and so on (*Ku Ntu or Kuntu*) are equally spirit expressions. As such everything and all being is *UbuNtu* and as such are more than simply related to each other. All that exists are different concrete expressions of *Ntu*. In effect, Being is being spirit in a reality of spirit. All being is therefore spirit, energy, or *UbuNtu*. In being, humans exist in the aforementioned categories. The category *Mu Ntu* includes intelligent beings that are living, the dwellers of the afterlife (dead), those yet-to-be-born as well as the orishas, loas, and ancestors. That which exists as *Ki Ntu* are forces that are activated at the command of *Mu Ntu*. Plants, animals, minerals, created objects, ideas, and so on are all spirit (*Ki Ntu*) awaiting the command or activation by *Mu Ntu*. Spirit also exists or expresses itself as space and time. This is *Ha Ntu*. The *UbuNtu* idea should be thought of as one of the root ideas in African philosophical thought and the further creation of a Pan African Black psychology.

As evolved, the Pan African Black psychology embraced the African meaning of being human as being spirit, an energy or power. Refashioning African philosophical thought with its *Kmt-Nubia/BaNtu-Kongo* grouping, as an African Grand Narrative would assert that human beings as Spirit Beings are those who live and move within and are inseparable from the ocean of waves or radiations of Spirit (energy). A human being is Spirit that affirms its humanity by recognizing the humanity of other spirits and on that basis establishes humane relations with them. A human being is Spirit whose unfolding is a constant and continual inquiry into its own being, experience, knowledge, and truth. To be human is to be Spirit in motion (unfolding). Being human is of perpetual, constant, and continual unfolding (vibration—sharing and exchanging) of Spirit. In this regard, Fu-Kiau (2001) clarifies that the human being is a "threefold unfolding" experience in the realms of yet-to-live, living, and after-living. He further notes that a human being is a living sun (energy), possessing "knowing and knowable" spirit (energy) through which spirit in human form has an enduring relationship with the total perceptible and ponderable universe.

Using indigenous epistemic reflections, cultural appreciations, and apperceptions about reality to inform their knowing framework and intellectual mindset, an African Grand Narrative as the mindset for guiding counseling and treatment would be a constructive process, reflecting deep intrinsic African beliefs as both descriptive and explanatory discourse by which Africans interpret and reinterpret their experiences in order to recognize, record, and make sense of events and experiences, especially wellness and *dis-at-ease*. The power of the grand narrative is that it shapes and influences what we see and accept as normal. The African Grand Narrative shapes and influences, without European or Western interference, what is understood to be and accepted as normal. The African epistemological method would allow indigenous African treatment and therapy to be guided by participation (equilibrium—balance between Knowing, Knower, and Known), relatedness (harmony), and unicity (balance between rationality and intuition; analyses and syntheses; known and unknown, and the visible and invisible).

African deep thought and wisdom traditions suggest that the Universe is "matter" in appearance, and "Spirit" in reality. The material universe is only the perception of reality, that is, in fact, nonlocalized, immutable, and eternal spirit. African epistemology, consequently, imprints the natural centrality of the role of the Divine and of the Spirit in the acquisition of knowledge.

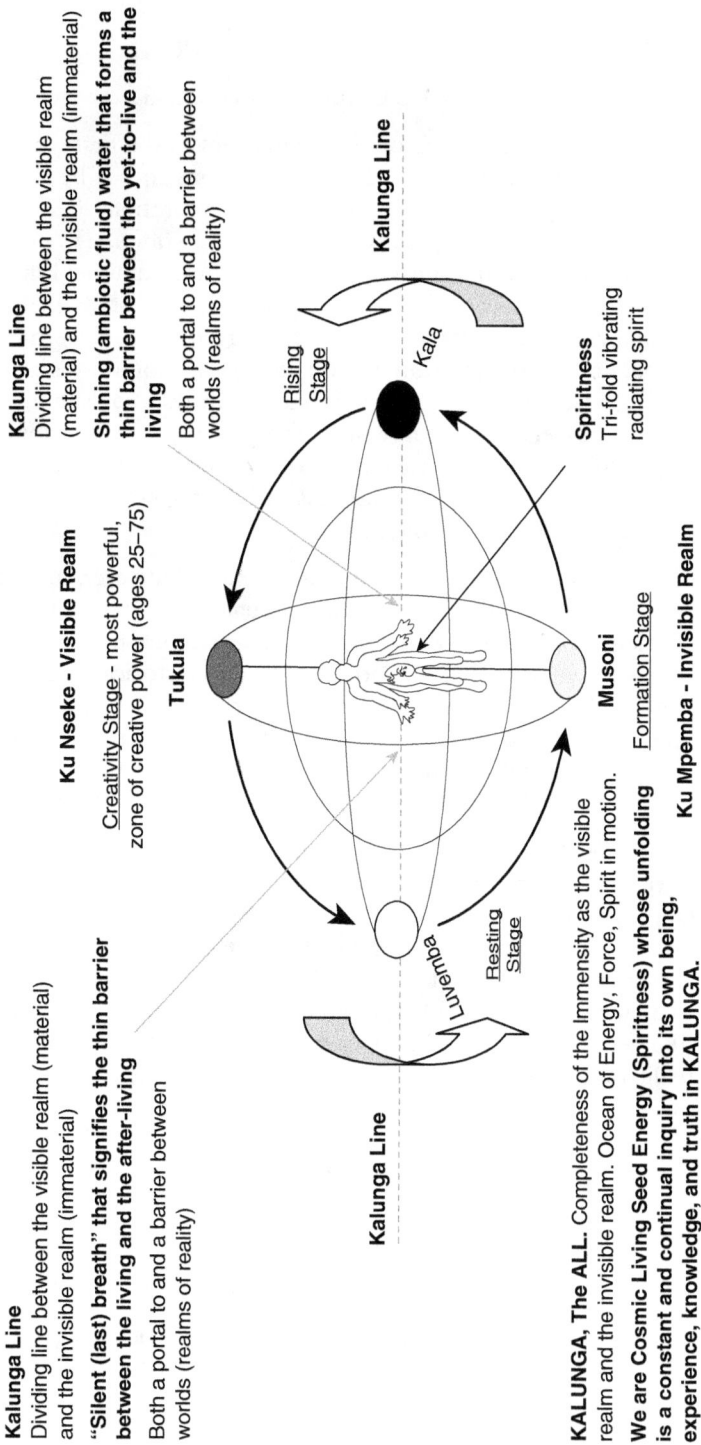

Dikenga Kongo Cosmos
(Four Moments of the Sun)

Kalunga Line

Dividing line between the visible realm (material)
and the invisible realm (immaterial)

**"Silent (last) breath" that signifies the thin barrier
between the living and the after-living**

Both a portal to and a barrier between
worlds (realms of reality)

Ku Nseke - Visible Realm

Creativity Stage - most powerful,
zone of creative power (ages 25–75)

Tukula

Kalunga Line

Dividing line between the visible realm
(material) and the invisible realm (immaterial)

**Shining (ambiotic fluid) water that forms a
thin barrier between the yet-to-live and the
living**

Both a portal to and a barrier between
worlds (realms of reality)

Spiritness

Tri-fold vibrating
radiating spirit

Kalunga Line

Kala

Rising
Stage

Luvemba

Resting
Stage

Musoni

Formation Stage

Ku Mpemba - Invisible Realm

Kalunga Line

KALUNGA, The ALL. Completeness of the Immensity as the visible
realm and the invisible realm. Ocean of Energy, Force, Spirit in motion.

**We are Cosmic Living Seed Energy (Spiritness) whose unfolding
is a constant and continual inquiry into its own being,
experience, knowledge, and truth in KALUNGA.**

Nobles, W. W. (2009–12) augmentation in collaboration with Kimwandende Kia Bunseke Fu-Kiau, *Simba Simbi: A Deep Insight Retreat Into Traditional African Systems of Health and Healing* (also see *Tying the Spiritual Knot: African Cosmology of the Bantu-Kongo*).

61

AFRICAN-CENTERED
LANGUAGE AND LOGIC

The borrowing and using of alien languages as the first tool of communication . . . is one of the most dangerous steps chosen by African people (Fu-Kiau, post mortum[8]). Too often, our exploration of African thought and behavior is conceptually incarcerated (Nobles, 1976) by the languages, concepts, and ideas we have inherited from our Euro-American psychological education. When we prioritize English as the language of communication, we carry the weight of Greco-Roman, Germanic, Anglo-Saxon, and Euro-American culture and civilization through our mouths, which, in turn, serve as containers and pathways to our minds and knowing. Language, and the knowing it represents, reflects a people's culture. When African people use non-African concepts (i.e., Greek, Roman, Anglo-Saxon), we unknowingly distort the phenomena associated with the reality identified by the concept.

The importance of language is fundamental. However, in rescuing concepts from traditional African languages, we are faced with the problematic issue of adopting replacement terms for ideations, that is, supervisor, intern, that are not part of our historical reality (memory). Nevertheless, I believe, it is only through the penetrating "reinterpretation" of the language and logic of our African ancestry that Africans (both continental and diasporan) will be able to rescue and remember our humanity, wholeness, and wellness and, in so doing, engage in the restoration of well-being.

With the languaging of Skh Djr, the Science of Being will utilize African language as the scientific terminology for the identification and understanding of African reality and phenomena. Accordingly, it is through African languaging that we can reinvent our own scientific terminology. The languaging of Skh Djr should utilize African language as the scientific terminology for the identification and understanding of African reality and phenomena.

ENDNOTES

1. Epistemic justice requires us to look at world population distribution and the domination of "thought." The African world has approximately 1 billion people (15% of the world's population), the second-most populated continent in the world. The Caribbean and Latin America combined has another 600 million people (9% of the world's population). The African World has about 24% of the world's population and Europe and America have only 17% of the world's population. Europe's population is 733 million people (12% of the world's population); with estimated 4% non-European would

adjust to 8% world population. North America (primarily consisting of the United States and Canada) has approximately 352 million people (5% of the world's population). Note: African Americans represent 0.132% of the U.S., thus adjusting North America to about 351,953,535 million people. Why should 17% of world's population's Grand Narrative dominate or influence the rest of the world, especially the African world? Why does Euro-American psychology dominate the understanding and interpretation of entire human family?

2. Returning to the source means returning to the epistemic grounded ideas that have not been locked in the prison of Plato's academy. It means facing Aristotle's ghost and seeing through Descartes's delusion.

3. Obenga vis-à-vis the origins of the universe from the *Book of the Dead*.

4. *Webster's New Dictionary* (1999)

5. *The Egyptian Book of the Dead*, by E. A Wallis Budge (1967, Dover Publications). Obenga's review of two books collected by the Dutch Egyptologist Adriaan A. de Buck titled *The Sarcophagus Texts* and the *Book of Two Ways* and discovered these extraordinary origins in Egyptian philosophy and Egyptian thought that "Beginning with this 'uncreated reality', the forms of creation were organized" the beginning of all beginnings was Nwn. This was the name given to the primal, absolute mass of water, container of all seed, home to all creative potential. This was a sort of an all-encompassing ocean, existing before any other form of life known to us. It predated all motion, as we understand it. It was reality before the universe we know, already pregnant with the "raw material" of creation in latent state. Here was the "chaotic" medium of incipient forms, the unshaped, pretemporal manifestation of the creator god. In the cosmology of the *Book of the Dead*, genesis was the construction of the cosmos in its present form. The process began with the primal waters, a reality older than the creator god, who emerged from these very primal waters. Indeed, it was within this "primordial chaos" that the demiurge achieved consciousness of self. Only after that rise to self-consciousness did the demiurge come into real existence, on its own and by itself. From the perspective of ancient Egyptian pharonic philosophy, then, all components of the world as it now is—goddesses, gods, and stars, sky and earth, the world of the living and the abode of the dead, in short, every dimension of existence—had a starting point, a genesis. The one exception was the *Nwn*, the absolute reality of the primal waters. The existence of *Nwn* was posited as such in its sheer absolute quality. *Nwn* was the uncreated reality of moist, watery, abyssal depths, fecundating and creative (pp. 45–46).

6. See Nobles (1997), *To Be African or Not to Be: The Question of Identity or Authenticity—Some Preliminary Thoughts*.

7. Embracing an Alien worldview results in loss of authority to socialize and enculturate according to one's own cultural precepts, the inability to self-generate and creativity (original), the failure to support one's own human imperative (procreation, sustenance, protection, recuperative time/space, and developmental guidelines), the failure to recognize relational essence (sense of

efficacy, intimacy and integrity, the engagement of mutated, distorted or contaminated practices, traditions and customs), and internalizing Kambon's Cultural Misorientation, Akbar's Personality Disorders, and Nobles's Shattered Consciousness and Fractured Identity.

8. Permission to cite and quote *Knowing About* (1984, unpublished) was given by Kenneth Nunn, 2021, K. Kia Bunseke Fu-Kiau's Executor.

V

Skh

The Science of the Being

The *Skh* as the science of the Being (Spirit) represents the ongoing struggle to free our thinking and practice from the constraints and limitations of Western orthodoxy and to rescue and refine African indigeneity as the praxis for the restoration of wellness with African American personhood, familyhood, and peoplehood. Embracing the *Skh* is an attempt to draw out the "mindscape" or intellectual terrain that must be traveled in order to understand the core "epistemic change" and "paradigmatic shifting" necessary for the creation of a culturally congruent (African-centered) program and praxis.[1]

Consistent with Diop's (1974) directive to examine the domains of history, language, and psyche, *Skh Djr* has allowed us to further interrogate the language and logic of classical Africa and rescue an uncontaminated process of knowing in order to gain insight into the functioning of contemporary African peoples. *Skh Djr* has been defined as the process of understanding, examining, and explicating the meaning, nature, and functioning of being human for African people by conducting a profound and penetrating search, study, and mastery of the process of "illuminating" the human spirit or essence, as well as all human experience and phenomena. It is further believed that to fully understand the complexity of the *Skh Djr* (illumination of the spirit) one must explore the African antecedent comprehension of what it means to be human or to be a person. In so doing, *Skh Djr* requires one to think deeply about African meanings and understandings about being human. To attend to the person is to attend to the Spirit. This can only be accomplished by interrogating the language and logic of traditional African peoples, which, in turn, will allow us to gain insight into the functioning of contemporary African peoples.

Previously, I suggested that *Skh Djr* was an advanced level of Pan African (Black) psychology. *Skh Djr* represents Black psychology's advancement to the status of the science of African human functioning. Further exploration requires the application of *Skh* (advanced African-centered/Black psychology) and the acceptance and utilization of an African episteme, worldview, and wisdom traditions, that will formally engage and apply African American cultural orientation, precepts, and technology to the service of the restoration of wellness.

The question of *Skh* as the Science of Being[2] must ultimately turn to the task of our being able to illuminate the spirit of *Mu Ntu* to the people worldwide. In furthering the challenge of Black psychology to rescue ancient African deep thought, it has been suggested that the adoption of *Skh Djr* is the process for understanding, examining, and explicating the meaning, nature, and functioning of being human for African people by conducting a deep, profound, and penetrating search, study, and mastery of the process of "illuminating" the human spirit is the basis for the science.

Skh, the Science of Being, therein proffers both a process, that is, *Skh Djr* for understanding, examining, and explicating the meaning, nature, and functioning of being human for African people by conducting a deep, profound and penetrating search, study, and mastery of the process of "illuminating" the human spirit or essence and a method, that is, *Irt hr Skh* that requires one to "clarify" human definition, meaning, and resolute position or purpose in the world; "analyze and describe" the concrete human conditions which affect and influence our collective human development and consciousness; and "prescribe and excite" solutions and actions that will free humanity from both material and spiritual degradation.

In order to fully understand the complexity of the *Skh Djr* (illumination of the spirit), one must include a discussion of the African comprehensive antecedent of what it means to be human or to be a person. To understand this point, one has to think deeply and profoundly about African meanings and understandings about being human. Our ancestors were spread throughout the diaspora absent of freedom, and put in chains. However, they did not arrive absent of language, thoughts, and beliefs about who they were. Our ancestors on the continent had a sacred relation to the land. However, because of colonial domination, that relationship was often disrupted. Our ancestors came with a language and a system of beliefs (logic) about what it means to be human and to whom and whose they were and why they existed. It is through a penetrating reinterpretation of the language and logic of our African ancestry that both continental and diasporan Africans will be able to rescue and remember our humanity, wholeness, and wellness. *Skh* requires that we embrace the African meaning of being human as being spirit, an energy or power, that is to say, a human being is spirit whose unfolding is a constant and continual inquiry into its own being, experience, knowledge, and truth. To be human, therefore, is to be spirit in motion (unfolding). Being human is perpetual, constant, and continual unfolding (vibration—sharing and exchanging) of spirit.

ONTOLOGICAL AND
PSYCHOLOGICAL INVARIANTS

It is important in the illumination of *Skh* to note that there are conditions or features that are permanent. These are ontological invariants that are metaphysical beliefs about the features or aspects of the nature of being and existence that are not liable to or capable of change. Given the Ancient African thought, one can see that ontologically, African belief systems understood that the nature of all things in the universe was the Ka of God (force), or "Spirit." It is logical or at least consistent that in believing that all things, including being, were endowed with the same vibrating, radiating unfolding spirit, one would also believe that all things are "essentially" one or the same. For Africans, therefore, our most invariant ideas about order (i.e., worldview) would be based on the ontological identification of "being (existence) in the universe" as being characterized by a cosmological "participation in the constant and continually unfolding spirit." Parenthetically, it is understandable that, if ontologically, the African believes that the nature of all things is spirit, then the African would view the variety of cosmic beings as quantitative alterations of the same Supreme Energy. This is the constant unchanging, though often unrecognized or disrespected, African belief.

Accordingly, the African conception of the world and the phenomena within it amounts to a set of syntheses (connections), separations (disconnections), and contradictions (antagonisms) as unfolding spirit "expressed" as a particular classification of beings and experienced as differential quantifications of force. Combined, these "connective" and "antagonistic" participatory sets form the whole of universal relations. Accordingly, relationships in the universe are determined by elements belonging to the same metaphysical plane, "participating by resemblance" or by elements belonging to different metaphysical planes, "participating by difference" (Thomas, 1961). The dynamic quality of the total universe is, however, thought to be the conciliation of these various "participatory sets." In fact, the conciliation of the unity of the cosmos and the diverseness of beings within the cosmos make for the invariant features (e.g., dynamism, interdependence, variety, optimism) of the traditional African worldview.

The *UbuNtu* idea or African "authentic core" is consistent with the idea of *Skh*. *UbuNtu* is composed of the belief that the person is human because there is an indisputable connection between the person and the *Kalunga* or the Supreme Being. In fact, the person is really seen as an undeniable expression or manifestation of God. Included in the authentic core is also the belief that (1) the complexity (immaterial and material) of the person gives one an intrinsic human value and (2) that the person is, in fact, a "process" characterized by the divinely governed laws of appearing, perfecting, and compassion, which are revealed within or through one's destiny. Another important common belief in the African authentic core is that harmony and balance between and within the supra-, inter-, and intra-worlds of the person are key to "being human." In effect, the BaNtu expansion which reflected a geographical distribution of the spread of language, culture, and spiritual beliefs, as well as farming, agriculture, civil society, and high culture, should also be viewed as the distribution of a BaNtu complex of ideas or the *UbuNtu* idea.

One of the distinct aspects of African spirit systems, as the illumination or expression of Spirit, is the recognition that to be human is to be Spirit that is in constant contact with the "spirit" powers which dwell in both the visible and invisible realm. To be human is to be a spirit force that is intricately connected or embedded in a differentiating structure of ever-expanding energy. This ever-expanding energy, the totality of which is the Supreme Being, requires that humans as spirit are capable of knowing self (intra), other human spirits (inter), and ultimately the Divine (supra). Given these beliefs and ideas, one could suggest that the meaning of being human was to be a knowing and knowable perpetually vibrating Spirit with a profound sense of excellence and appropriateness and whose relationship and purpose in the world (both visible and invisible realms) is to be the cause and consequence of joy and beauty.

Psychologically speaking or in terms of social life, individual consciousness becomes such that the familyhood constituted the reference point wherein one's existence was perceived as being interconnected to the existence of all else. The individual was an integral part of the collective unity, that is, the family. In recognition of this kind of awareness, others (Mbiti, 1970) have noted that the traditional African view of "self" is contingent upon the existence of and interconnectedness with others (The Oneness of Being). This is an African psychological invariant.

The threefold unfolding (yet-to-live, living, and after-living) of Spirit can be thought of as the "essentiality-of-being" and invariably suggests that existence is at the level of family or peoplehood which is more permanent and continuous than individual existence. Existence is, therefore, at the level of the family or peoplehood. The family essence or essence of familyhood precedes the individual essence. The family or peoplehood is the center of existence. It is the center of the universe. The essentiality-of-being, which includes beings yet-to-live, the living, and dwellers in the after-life, is the psychological invariant that serves as the essence of the familyhood and must be kept alive. Our family then becomes the source of our definition.

While not always reflected in the social constructions and behavioral representations characteristic of a particular people, African invariants, nevertheless, do exist and may very well be the source of existential tensions and crises in being human due to Westernization and the hegemony of White supremacy.

AFRICAN REALMS OF REALITY AND EPISTEME

The utilization of an African episteme, worldview, and wisdom traditions is necessary to understand the *Skh* and requires a brief discussion of traditional African beliefs about the real(ity) and its formation. The BaNtu-Kongo[3] believe that the heated force of *Kalunga* blew up and down as a huge storm of projectiles, *kimbwandende*, fusing together a huge mass. In the process of cooling, solidification of the fused mass occurs, giving birth to the Earth (Fu-Kiau, 2001). In effect, the BaNtu believe that all of reality (*Kalunga*) is fundamentally a process of perpetual and mutual sending and receiving of spirit (energy) in the form of waves and radiations. *Kalunga* or reality is the totality, the completeness of all life. It is an ocean of energy, a force in motion. *Kalunga* is everything, sharing life and becoming life continually after life itself. As the totality or the complete living, *Kalunga* comprises both a visible realm (*ku nseke*) and an invisible realm (*ku mpemba*). The visible physical world has spirit (energy) as its most important element or nature. Referred to as *nkisi* (medicine), the spirit element of the physical (visible) world has the power to care, cure, heal, and guide. The material universe is only the perception of real(ity), that is, in fact, nonlocalized, immutable, and eternal Spirit. As the totality or the complete living what is real(ity) (*Kalunga*) composes both a visible realm (*Ku Nseke, Aye*) and an invisible realm (*Ku Mpemba, Orun*). The visible realm is considered the "microcosmos," the immediate perceptible world. The invisible realm is considered the "mesocosmos," the intermediate world of spirits, genies, and beneficial and malevolent forces. The "macrocosmos," the world beyond the senses, is the realm of the Divine, ancestors, and spirit beings. Reality consists of the visible and the invisible, with the invisible being far greater than the visible. The invisible (spiritual) world (*ku mpemba*) is composed of human experience, ancestor experience, and the soul–mind experience. The *ku mpemba* has Spirit (energy) as its most important element or nature. In effect, if reality (visible and invisible) is, it is Spirit. All that exists are, therefore, different concrete expressions of Spirit. In effect, Being is being Spirit in a reality of spirit. Fu-Kiau (2001) further clarifies that the human being or *muntu* is a "threefold unfolding" experience in the realms of yet-to-live, living, and after-living. He further notes that a human being is a living sun (energy), possessing "knowing and knowable" Spirit (energy) through which spirit in human form has an enduring relationship with the total perceptible and ponderable universe. The BaNtu-Kongo believe that diverse forces and waves of energy that govern life surround humans. This fire force called *kalunga* is complete in and of itself and emerges within the emptiness or nothingness and becomes the source of life on earth.

African deep thought and wisdom traditions suggest that the Universe is "matter" in appearance, and "Spirit" in reality. The material universe is only the perception of reality, that is, in fact, nonlocalized, immutable, and eternal spirit. African epistemology, consequently, imprints the natural centrality of the role of the Divine and of the Spirit in the acquisition of knowledge.

Accordingly, the fundamental ideas about the meaning of being human and how we come to "Be" and knowing our purpose is essential. The *BaNtu-Kongo* geneses story (Fu-Kiau, 2001) says that *Kalunga* the totality, the completeness of all life is an ocean of energy, a Spirit (force) in motion that is everything, sharing life and becoming life continually after life itself. *Kalunga* (energy/spirit) whose unfolding is a constant and continual inquiry into its own being, experience, knowledge, and truth of yet-to-be, living, and after-living. As genesis, a person is a second sun rising and setting around the earth to *Kala*, to be, become, and illuminate.

Being human is being Spirit, energy, or power. Being Spirit is to be a spirit being (not a human being) and to be one who lives and moves within and is inseparable from the ocean of waves and radiations of Spirit (energy or power). This condition I have defined as "spiritness."[4] A spirit being is one (Spirit) who affirms one's being by recognizing the beingness of others and on that basis establishes affirming relations with them. A so-called human being is actually Spirit whose unfolding is a constant and continual inquiry into its own being, experience, knowledge, and truth (Ramose, 1991). To be human is to be a Spirit in motion (unfolding). Being human, as Spirit, is being a phenomenon of perpetual, constant, and continual unfolding (vibration—sharing and exchanging) of life spirit. Humans are containers and instruments of Divine spirit and relationships. A human being, as Spirit, is akin to a living sun (unlimited power), possessing a knowing and knowable spirit (energy or power) through which one has an enduring relationship with the total perceptible and ponderable universe. The spirit being is a trifold unfolding experience of yet-to-live, living, and after-living Spirit. All that exists are, therefore, different concrete expressions of *Ntu* (Spirit).

As mentioned above, the BaNtu-Kongo people believe that the person is an energy, Spirit, or power. And as a Spirit, the person is a phenomenon of "perpetual veneration." The person is both the container and instrument of Divine energy and relationships. Consistent with the Mali notion *wayne bibi,* to be human for the BaNtu-Kongo is to be a person who is a living (Black) sun, possessing a knowing and knowable Spirit (energy) through which one has an enduring relationship with the total perceptible and ponderable universe.

The African-centered understanding of Spiritness may need further explication. Spirit (*Ntu*) is the energy, force, or power that is both the inner essence and the outer envelope of all of reality. As energy, Spirit becomes *Spiritness* and therein serves to ignite and enliven the human state of being. *Spiritness* pertains to the condition of actually being Spirit. It is both a metaphysical state and an ethereal extension or connection into and between the *supra world* of the Deities, the *interworld* of other beings, and the *inner world* of the self. In the African-centered paradigm, illumination of the Human Spirit, or *Spiritness*, is the quintessential aspect of our beingness.

It is more than the "life force" (breath, soul, essence) that enlivens human beings. It is that which is essential to being for everything. The notion of Spirit or force or power makes no distinction between Spirit and matter. Matter and Spirit are not separate. They are not different or apart. Reality is not a duality of matter and Spirit. *UbuNtu* is all that is or Be. Conceptually, *Ntu* is a modal point at which being assumes concrete form. *Ntu* is reflected in four categories of expression in BaNtu philosophy. In effect, there is one essence with four categories of expression. Spirit is the essence of all and the visible (material) reality is simply the manifestation of the invisible. Human beings are more correctly spirit beings. They are those who live and move within and are inseparable from the ocean of waves and radiations of spirit (energy). *Spiritness* pertains to being Spirit. As such, Spirit beings or *Spiritness* has the quality of being or reflecting spirit as (1) retention Spirit (energy): the act or power of "remembering" or retaining an aspect, feature, or part of something or idea; (2) residual Spirit (energy): the act or power that constitutes the residue or remainder of an original form or process; the remaining value after repeated usage; (3) resonant Spirit (energy): the state of a system in which a vibration or energy field is produced in response to an external stimulus; resonance occurs when the characteristics or qualities of an external or neighboring system or subject are the same or nearly the same as the qualities or features of the target system; resonance can be seen as reflections, reverberations, spontaneous recall or memory; (4) romance

Spirit (energy): a state or condition wherein one holds, values, and treasures another with love, caring, and affection in order to sustain, promote, nurture, and inspire their "perfectibility"; romance is self- and collective cherishment; it is the essential act of personal preservation and collective actualization; and (5) reverberation Spirit (energy): the persistence of a phenomenon or act (like sound) after it has been cut off from its source (after its source has stopped); it is believed to be caused by multiple reflections of the thing (phenomena) in a closed space.

Consistent with *Skh*, consciousness would be (re)defined as a huge complex of Astral (Divine) energy in the form of Sensorial Informational Ideations.[5] In defining the term *consciousness* in this way, the immediate task is to free our thinking from the "meanings and constraints" imposed by our training in Western thoughts and techniques and especially by the Western episteme and paradigms that we have inherited for thinking itself. The African heritage of Black people is replete with elegant, elaborate, and extraordinary conceptualizations of human knowing and awareness. The following explication is a brief and partial composite of African-centered understanding of consciousness.

Consciousness relative to African people is, in effect, a construct that represents the ability of beings to know, perceive, understand, and be aware of self in relation to self and all else. All that is consciousness is revealed in (illumination, ergo *Skh*) and determined by relationships (energy in motion). At the most fundamental level, consciousness is found in the "pulse" that gives us life. A heart cell, for example, is unique in that it produces a strong electromagnetic signal that "radiates" (relates to) out beyond itself. The electromagnetic (EM) field produced by the heart radiates outward some 12 to 15 feet beyond our bodies. In effect, we are in constant contact or relationship with other human beings and energy-vibrating life forms at all times. One, in fact, can take two live heart cells, keep them apart and when they begin to die, as evidenced by fibrillation, bring them into close proximity to each other and they will resume their regular life-producing pulsation. Rhythmic sound can, in fact, connect us together.[6] Not only is cellular relationship indicated here, but the awareness and understanding (consciousness) of each cell to each other cell is evidence of and critical to life. What is most important here is that what is seen as the electromagnetic (EM) energy of the cells is, in fact, the consciousness of each cell that carries information or awareness. It is the "vibration" of each cell that results in the awareness of self (one cell) and other (another cell). Consciousness is, in effect, the intelligent energy of the Divine.

What the ancient Africans of the Nile Valley (Kemites) called the "Intelligence of the Heart" was, in fact, an intricate dialogue between the electromagnetic fields generated by the "knowing" cells in our physical manifestations of spirit,[7] for example, heart, mind, and skin and the electromagnetic energy fields in the world at large and selected energy fields found in our particular experience with time, place, and space. African beings can be distinguished by a particular consciousness that is reflected in a special capacity for having "intelligence" of the "mind and heart." In the many different physical manifestations of spirit, consciousness as spirit is inscribed in and determines the nature of every organism. Each animal, each species of plant, each mineral, and each of their respective components represent conscious energy vibrating at different speeds. Consciousness is, however, more than potentiality contained in itself. As a knowing and knowable spirit vibration, motion, or energy, consciousness is simultaneously "potentiality" and "intentionality" contained in the pulse of life.

At the human level, consciousness as spirit is always a collective experience and passes from one collective generation (Being) to the next. Like the energy or vibration indicative of it, consciousness is never destroyed. In fact, it is the reincarnation of consciousness, as Spirit, that constitutes the reincarnation of a person. A reincarnated person is a new person only in the carnal sense. The collective consciousness or what some call racial consciousness is constantly renewed in each succeeding generation. The reincarnated are different from the preceding generation only to the extent that the consciousness of the "next" generation vibrates at a new (different) speed. African people, as a particular vibratory phenomenon, reincarnate consciousness from one generation to the next irrespective of geographical location. Many of the great deep thinkers throughout the African world have spoken through this sense of consciousness, this force in motion, a consciousness that is in-born. Higgins (1994) noted that "We are Africans not because we are born in Africa, but because Africa is born in us." The Africa born in us is that in-born sense of consciousness, that vibratory fire force in motion that is complete in and of itself yet continually emerging to become the source and the consequence of living.

Consciousness is, therefore, the essence, energy, expression, and experience of Spirit (being) in the form of awareness, knowing, comprehension, and existing (being). It is that which allows African people to reflect, respond, project, and create from before and beyond the time of one's experiences. Having an awareness of oneself as Spirit in turn allows one to access realms of knowing that are not limited to just cognition or perception. It also allows one to be accessible to those Spirits in the realm of the Spirit. It connects knowing and awareness to both the perceivable (visible) and the unperceivable (invisible). Hence, consciousness as or driven by an eternal living Spirit is not bound by time, space, or place. It connects knowing, awareness, and comprehension to the universal and the Divine. Consciousness is, therefore, that which gives congruity between the supra-, inter-, and inner realms of being. It allows for the retention of ancestral sensibilities that interpret and give meaning to contemporary experience. It is consciousness, as awareness, as knowing and knowable, and its subsequent meaning that gives particular content, context, and contour to Black character and style. The desire to always function at a higher level (the sense of excellence) is characteristic of the consciousness as spirit energy of African people from time immemorial.

KNOWING AND KNOWABLE SPIRITNESS:
LIVING LIGHT (BIOPHOTONS)

The *UbuNtu* idea should be thought of as one of the root ideas in African philosophical thought and wisdom traditions. African wisdom traditions, especially the BaNtu-Kongo, teach that as Spirit beings we have an indelible and enduring relationship with both the visible and invisible realms of all of reality. Ntu is thought to be the universal expression of spirit or spirit. Ntu inseparable from Umu is Being itself. It is the cosmic universal force. *UbuNtu* is spirit in which Being and beings coalesce.

The similarity between contemporary scientific ideas and Ancient African thought is intriguing if not compelling. Ancient African ideas about being as energy are antecedent to the modern quantum physics notion of biophoton by minimally a thousand years, the African understanding of *Ntu* purports that spirit is knowing and knowable and as energy is living. Hence, the African knowing and knowable spirit (energy) is living (bio) light (photon). Accordingly, as a biophoton (living light) existing in the realms of the invisible (yet-to-live and after-living) and the visible (living), the knowing and knowable spirit is vibrating and radiating energy that is capable of emitting biophoton signals across and between realms of reality.[8]

Quantum mechanics has been able to demonstrate that not only do experiences affect the present, but future events can also bring about changes in present reality. The importance and impact of the observer in any given reality is that reality changes (Heisenberg uncertainty principle) when it is observed. If or when an observer changes how they think about or perceive a certain reality, that reality changes along with it. Entities from a common source remain connected even if they are separate. What happens to one is immediately reflected in the other (the law of consubstantiation). An essential African belief, if not law, is that relationships between entities are more important than their separate identities. The entire universe is interconnected. Bohm (2012) considered that what we take for reality are "surface phenomena, explicate forms that have temporarily unfolded out of an underlying implicate order." That is, the implicate order is the ground from which reality emerges.

Each contains the other two, with matter containing (energy and meaning); energy containing (matter and meaning) and meaning containing (matter and energy). Truth is not a two-dimensional image but multidimensional as a hologram with each component (matter, energy, meaning) capable of representing the whole and requiring the whole to make sense (Clegg, pp. 12–15). Quantum particles can act as particles, located in a single place, or they can act as waves scattered through space or in several places at once, ergo, in several places at once.[9] Like attracts like. Everything is vibrating energy that is understood and shaped by the meaning given to it through our thoughts and actions.

Quantum mechanics is preceded by African thought in almost every way. A core tenant of quantum physics is that there is a wave-like ocean of "possibilities" at the very basic level of matter (Smith, 2002, p. 5). Quantum mechanics has been able to demonstrate that not only does past experience affect the present and future events, but it can also bring about changes in present reality. Reality changes when it is observed; if and when an observer changes how they think and perceive a certain reality, that reality changes along with it.

Using subatomic particles as subset, it was discovered that particles could change from particle to waveform and then back again. They can leave one dimension and return back into it again (particle–wave duality). We influenced the very fabric of life by thinking about it (law of attraction, Smith, 2020, p. 11). Entities from a common source remain connected even if they are separate. What happens to one is immediately reflected in the other. "Relationships" between entities are more important than their separate identities. The entire universe is interconnected.

Bohm (2012) suggested that reality is not just made up of matter energy but of matter (the explicit order), energy (the implicit order), and meaning (the super implicit order). Each contains the other two with matter containing (energy and meaning), energy containing (matter and meaning), and meaning containing (matter and energy). Bohm considered that what we take for reality are "surface phenomena, explicate forms that have temporarily unfolded out of an underlying implicate order." That is, the implicate order is the ground from which reality emerges.

Truth is not a two-dimensional image but multidimensional as a hologram with each component (matter, energy, meaning) capable of representing the whole and requiring the whole to make sense.

Quantum particles can act as particles, located in a single place, or they can act as waves scattered through space or in several places at once, ergo in several places at once, ergo "Schrödinger's cat" (quantum mystery) in which the cat is left dead and alive at the same time. Quantum particles seem to affect each other instantaneously even if they are far away from each other (Einstein's spooky behavior at a distance). Quantum coherence in the law of attraction suggests that like attracts like; everything is vibrating energy that is understood and shaped by the meaning given to it through our thoughts and actions. We manifest reality according to quantum physics; in the law of attraction people are the creators of their own universe. Einstein's famous formula, $E = mc^2$, explains the relationship between energy and matter. All that exists in the universe is energy, and energy is ever evolving. In cryptic form, the idea of be(ing) recognizes that *to be* is fundamental to existence and far more significant than *doing* (conative), *feeling* (affective), and *thinking* (cognitive). Essentially, if you don't be, then all else and everything else is non-existence.

ANCESTRAL CONSCIOUSNESS

Understanding ancestral consciousness and its role in speaking to the invisible requires a brief discussion of autopoiesis, noetic sensoria, and symbolic thinking. It is believed that Homo erectus (1.8 million years ago) possessed a brain of sufficient size to be capable of elementary symbolic thought. Symbolic thinking, in turn, is associated with the emergence of the (un)conscious mind in the hominid lineage. Energy exchange is in some way connected to the origin of human consciousness. In possessing symbolic thought, ancient Spirit beings, so-called Homo erectus, are thought to have been capable of initiating the practice of magical or proto-religious rituals (time, rhythm, and motion). Rituals involving rhythmic movement of energy (Spirit), in turn, fostered or altered perceptual states leading to the "numinous" mind. Nascent numinous mind represents awareness of a metaphysical order and evidence of a specialized and complex form of symbolic thinking. This metaphysical perception signaled a shift in "noetic" outlook toward oneself and others that is an inner sensory experience, that is, consciousness as Spirit. Noetic sensoria promoted a (cognitive) context for so-called psycho-cultural transformation that is conducive to abstract thinking and feeling, as well as existential inquiry. Noetic sensoria evolving over hundreds of millennia arguably could have been selected for the biological changes that led to an enlarged and refined hominid brain capacity capable of "ratiocination" or comparative thinking (consciousness). Noetic sensoria can be seen in most African (Kemetic,[10] Akan,[11] Yoruba,[12] Sonay,[13] Mende,[14] KiZulu,[15] BaNtu[16]) conceptualizations of being and consciousness. Ultimately, African deep thought and wisdom traditions regarding being and consciousness support the idea that the Universe is matter in appearance, and spirit in reality. The material universe is only the perception of reality, that is nonlocalized, immutable, and eternal Spirit. African epistemology, consequently, imprints the natural centrality of the role of the Divine and of the Spirit in the acquisition of knowledge (Viriri &

Mungwini, 2010). "Ancestral Time" is, therefore, the simultaneous presence of energy events in what Mbiti (1990) called the *Sasa* and *Zamani*. We are our Ancestors. The ancestors continually send offer waves to both the living and the yet-to-be-born. We are in constant quantum transactions with ourselves (the living, the ancestors, the yet-to-be-born). What is seen as the human soul is the spirit of God. Consciousness as Spirit is both the substance (essence) and state of all that exists and does not exist. It is the capacity to absorb all life (energy) and information. It is more than being simply aware. It is being aware, unaware, and beyond awareness at the same time. Consciousness is the essence, energy, expression, and experience of being as the material (physical) and mental (nonphysical) reflection of spirit and the vibratory evidence and energy of the Divine All. Consciousness is that which transcends thought and penetrates (absorbs) everything so as to make being aware of itself.

We (the yet-to-be-born, the living, and the after-living) are all Spirit (energy). In the field of holographic subquantum physics (Malklaka, 2015) there is no such thing as solid matter. Solid matter is, in reality, nothing but lots of empty space and energy fields. All that exists in this universe is energy, and energy is ever evolving. Mainstream physicists now accept that there are only "force (energy) fields" pushing against each other, giving the illusion of solidity. All that exists in this universe is energy or Spirit. Current thinking suggests that the entire universe is a holographic projection (construct) with what is considered matter being an illusion. Within this conception, it is posited a tripartite universe: (1) subquantum *pixel grid*—the primary level of incompressible physical space, (2) subquantum *vortices* (ether)—intermediary level between the pixel grid and fundamental particles, and (3) the smallest *fundamental particles*.

Western science is now moving toward the idea that the universe behaves intelligently and that there is a source of energy that shapes it. Dr. Finch, in his book *The Star of Deep Beginnings: The Genesis of African Science and Technology* (1998), notes that in quantum physics, time can flow in one direction as easily as another. The implication of this thinking is almost mind-boggling. Every observation is both a start of a wave propagated toward the future in search of a receiver event and is itself the receiver of a wave that has propagated toward it from some past observation event. In other words, every observation, every act of conscious awareness sends out both a wave toward the future and a wave toward the past. It is the future with the strongest wave match for its past that combines with the offer wave from the past to create the present event. Defying comprehension, this may be the process, offer and echo waves, that may be the medium for communication between the dwellers in the visible and invisible realms. Quantum physics (Tyson, 2004) now recognizes what our ancient ones knew regarding being and consciousness:

nothing is set. There are no limits. Everything is vibrating energy embedded in our noetic sensoria. The physics of possibilities allows for ancestral consciousness. To sum up, quantum physicists (Clegg, 2019) say the objective material world is an illusion and that the universe is made up of dark matter, dark energy, and subatomic particles in the form of matter and "stuff" that fills the void or gaps between matter. The void or gap may be ancestral or quantum consciousness (Finch, 1998, pp. 261–270) as revealed in African noetic sensoria.

Consider, for instance, as noetic sensoria, ancestral consciousness as spirit is essentially part of *Kalunga* (the All, the Never-Ending, Boundless Totality). It is "astral forces and waves of energy" reflected as universal laws of creation that govern life. It is divine energy made manifest. It is well accepted that neural communication is mediated by bioelectricity and chemical molecules via the processes called bioelectrical and chemical transmission, respectively. Cell-to-cell communication by biophotons, also called ultra-weak photon emissions, has been demonstrated in several plants, bacteria, and certain animal cells. Biophotons may play a potential role in neural signal transmission and processing, contributing to the understanding of the basic functions of the nervous system such as perception, learning and memory, emotion, and consciousness. Ancestral consciousness as spirit is the essence, energy, expression, and experience of noetic sensoria's capacity as a living system to continually exchange knowing and knowable energy between realms of reality.

Concluding Consideration: To be human is to be Spirit (African Deep Thought). The human spirit is energy and while NOT limited to just the physical analyses of energy, Spirit does, in part, function according to the laws of quantum physics. The *living*, the *dead* (ancestors), and those *yet-to-be-born* can be considered "energy events" in time. As particles, energy events once connected to one another will continue to interact even at distances of light years apart (Bell's inequality). Two or more energy events (the living, the ancestors, the yet-to-be-born) connected by "synchronicity" are capable of collapsing time and space (Jung's synchronicity—nonlocality, Einstein's "Spooky action at a distance"). Every act of conscious awareness sends out both "offer" and "echo" waves toward the future and toward the past. Consciousness as Spirit has the capacity to transcend (collapse) time and continually exchange energy (Spirit) into matter (the physical).

Consciousness as spirit relative to African people is, in effect, a construct that represents the ability of human beings to know, perceive, understand, and be aware of self in relation to self and all else. Consciousness as spirit is revealed in and determined by energy in motion (relationships). Everything vibrates in a Divinely governed Universe. Consciousness is "potentiality" contained in itself. As potentiality contained in itself, the entire (multi)universe, as a never-ending totality of possibilities, is consciousness. Consciousness as Spirit is, in effect, the intelligent energy of the Divine.

Consciousness and identity are inextricably connected. Consciousness is awareness of all (looking out onto everything). Identity is how all is aware of you (how looked upon). Identity is how a Being is recognized and locatable in time and including the meaning, value, and worth given to or accepted by that designation and determination. Included in the African notion of identity is the belief that the complexity (immaterial and material) of being "a person" gives one an intrinsic human value and that the person is, in fact, a process characterized by the divinely governed laws of essence, appearance, perfection, and compassion.

The spectrum of consciousness includes numerous levels, which differ in degree of frequency and density. In fact, the level of consciousness determines the configuration of matter. Level is indicated by vibration. Each animal, each species of plant, each mineral, and each of their respective components represent conscious energy vibrating at different speeds. Consciousness is inscribed in and determines the nature of every organism. Consciousness is, however, more than self-contained potentiality. As a knowing and knowable vibration, motion, or energy, consciousness is simultaneously potentiality and intentionality contained in the pulse of life itself. Like the energy or vibration indicative of it, consciousness is never destroyed. It is the essence, energy, expression, and experience of Spirit (Being) in the form of awareness, knowing, comprehension, and existing (being). It is that which allows human beings to reflect, respond, project, and create from, before, and beyond the time of one's experiences. Consciousness is intricately merged with spirit. It is the "knowing" of what a knowing and knowable Spirit knows. It is the hermeneutics of consciousness that determines or allows African peoples to conceive of themselves with the understanding of being fundamentally spirit. Having an awareness of oneself as spirit allows one to access realms of knowing that are not limited to just cognition or perception. It also allows one to be accessible to those spirits in the realm of the spirit. It connects knowing and awareness to both the perceivable (visible) and the unperceivable (invisible). Hence, consciousness as an eternal living Spirit is not bound by time, space, or place. It connects knowing, awareness, and comprehension to the universal and the Divine. Consciousness is that which gives congruity between the supra-, inter-, and inner realms of being. Accordingly, it is consciousness that allows for the retention of ancestral sensibilities that interpret and give meaning to contemporary experience. Consciousness functions as both retentive and residual knowing and awareness. As retentive energy, consciousness allows for the remembering or retention of all previous information, experiences, and ideas. As residual energy, consciousness provides a conduit or circuit for tapping into the residue of human knowing and awareness and thereby creates or inspires new knowing and awareness. It is consciousness, as awareness, knowing, and comprehension, and its subsequent meaning that gives particular content, context, and contour to African character and style. The desire to always function at a higher level (the sense of excellence) is characteristic of the consciousness of African people from time immemorial.

Ultimately, the problem with identity is that it represents only a limited (albeit damaged) aspect of what it means "to be African." Black Identity[17] theory is, for the most part, founded upon an unwarranted acceptance of the Western (a.k.a. White supremacy) notions of human functioning with African peoples living in an anti-African reality. And like Horton's precepts on theory suggests, these "puzzling observations" about African American identity range from the reactions to de-Africanization and the hegemonic domination of White aesthetics and existence to creative responses to re-Africanizing and reinventing African American culture and traditions. In terms of the African ethos, then the first order or guiding belief (one with nature) suggests that African peoples believe themselves to be part of the natural rhythm of nature. The second order or guiding principle (survival of the tribe) suggests that African peoples believe in the cosmological and ontological importance of life, which in turn says that a people is "paramount" and "permanent." In accordance with the notions of one with nature and survival of the tribe, the African consequently thinks of experience as an intense complementary rhythmic connection or synthesis between the person and reality.

The cardinal point in understanding the traditional African conception of self is the belief that "I am because We are, and because We are, therefore I am" (Mbiti, 1970). Descriptively, we have defined this relationship (the interdependence of African peoples) as the orthodoxy of Oneness.

In recognizing that in terms of self-conception, the relationship of interdependence (and oneness of being) translates to an "extended" definition, we note again that the African feels themselves as part of all other African peoples or their tribe. One's self-definition is dependent upon the corporate definition of one's people. In effect, the people definition TRANSCENDS the individual definition of self, and the individual conception of self EXTENDS to include one's self and kind. This transcendent relationship is the "extended-self." The notion of the "we" instead of the "I" may become clearer through the following ontological analysis of the self. It is generally safe to say that the establishment of self is accomplished by (1) recognizing qualities or characteristics similar to one's own and/or (2) denying qualities and/or characteristics similar to one's own and/or to other people. The meaning that one has for being one within themselves and their universe (oneness of being) or what is felt as an inner feeling of oneness with oneself is the result of an interpretive process that evolved over the course of hundreds of millions of years. This inner "something" which is called the self is, in fact, the result of an evolutionary production, which in the end left one believing in the consistency of one's own internalized organized system. The evolution and consistency of the internalized systems of varying groups of people are not, however, always the same.

The philosophical notion of the oneness of being, for instance, is predicated on person being an integrated and indispensable part of the universe. For the African, the oneness of being suggests that humans participate in social space and elastic time as determined by the character of the universe. Hence, it is true that one's being is possible because of one's historical past as well as anticipated historical future. In an existential manner, therefore, having recognized the historical grounding of one's being, one also accepts the collective and social history of one's people. African people realize that one's self is not contained only in one's physical being and finite time. The notion of interdependence and oneness of being allows for a conception of self, which transcends through the historical consciousness of one's people, the finiteness of the physical body, finite space, and absolute time.

Self-awareness or self-conception is not, therefore, just the cognitive awareness of one's uniqueness, individuality, and historical finiteness. It is, in the African tradition, awareness of self as the awareness of one's historical consciousness (collective spirituality) and the subsequent sense of "we" or being one. It is in this sense that the self is portrayed as a TRANSCENDENCE INTO EXTENDATION. That is, the conception of self transcends and extends into the collective consciousness of one's people.

In African deep thought consistent with the *UbuNtu* idea, the concept of "being-becoming" as a singular construct or whole entity requires a different conception of Being. It suggests that the task of being is to continually become. The ideas of being and becoming are inseparable. It is one entity, a BeingBecoming. BeingBecoming is to be a Spirit in motion (unfolding). It is a being living and moving within an ocean of waves and radiations of spirit (energy). It is a living-dying-living system of systems and patterns of patterns of being. It is a knowing and knowable perpetually vibrating unfolding spirit. Similarly, consciousness and identity are likewise perpetually vibrating unfolding Spirit.

Consistent with these ideas is the need for a definition of *Skh* as the science of Being. Guided by the informative character of African deep thought, and the application and relevance of these ideas and notions in illuminating the Spirit, as noted, the notion of *Skh* requires that one interrogate the language and logic of traditional African people in order to gain insight into the functioning of contemporary African peoples. Traditional language is particularly important because in the language of traditional philosophy are found ancient words and phrases that illuminate the Spirit. It is through the penetrating reinterpretation of the language and logic of our African ancestry that Africans (both continental and diasporan) will be able to rescue and remember our humanity, wholeness, and wellness. Consciousness as Spirit is *Skh* and *Skh* is the Science of Being.

The ascension to *Skh*, therefore, requires a revision of the ABPsi definition of Black psychology. I propose that the formal definition of *Skh Djr* as the Science of Being be as follows: *Skh* represents the rescue and refinement of the recognition that a full understanding of reality acknowledges that Spirit is the basis of all that is known, unknown, and knowable. As the Science of Being, *Skh* is the penetrating search, study, and understanding that requires an approach that always seeks the deeper meaning of phenomena and explores the visible and invisible aspects of reality. As science, *Skh* is the dynamic manifestation of unifying African principles, values, and traditional thought regarding the illumination of the Spirit of Being. It is the self-conscious centering that examines the process that allows for the illumination and liberation of the Spirit. Relying on the principles of harmony within the universe as the Divinely ordered existence, *Skh* recognizes Spirit to be and permeate everything that is; the notion that everything in the universe is interconnected. The collective is the most salient element of existence, and the idea that communal sentience is the key to wellness and wholeness. *Skh Djr* is ultimately concerned with illuminating Be(ing); the meaning of existence; features of functioning; and the restoration, refinement, and promotion of development.

Skh Djr as defined requires us to further explore the different realms of reality, and the question of the invisible becomes an immanent concern. How is it known? What constitutes being in or within the invisible? How do the dwellers in the invisible connect to or communicate with the inhabitants of the visible realm? In effect, how do we "speak to the invisible"? All of these and many more interrogatories must be explored if we are to fully appreciate the African sense of Being.

One possibility may be found in what is called dream walking or dreaming. Freeing ourselves from the distortions emanating from the imposition of Judeo-Christian theology and the ghost of Greco-Roman hegemonic thought is no better illustrated than the airing of Pat Robertson's *The 700 Club* (November 17, 2021) conversation with a listener from his audience. His listener asked if, after someone dies, does God allow him to come back and visit us? I have personally experienced times when

I felt my mom's presence and observed things happening around me which led me to believe she is around me. What does the Bible say about this? Robertson said that the Bible talks about listening to spirits that peep and mutter but not turning to the living God. There are such things as familiar spirits and they have to do with family. They are part of it, but they're evil spirits, demonic spirits who play as if their departed grandmother mother or their brother or what-have-you and you know all I can say is the Bible is against it and these are demonic spirits, don't listen to them.

African cultural worldviews, on the contrary, emphasize the dynamic interrelatedness of all life through the ancestral source of infinite spiritual astral energy (see Bojuwoye & Edwards, 2011). This interrelatedness is a relationship with the ancestors and through the ancestors with the Divine (God) that permeates all being (p. 378). By escaping the ghost of the Greeks, an African episteme allows us to see that this dynamic interrelatedness is not between the Divine and humans but a seamless blending of the knowing and knowable energy (Spirit) between realms of reality as expressions of living and after-living. As an expression of consciousness, the ancestors (as energy events) continue to interact with the living. Communication between the realms (visible and invisible) of reality, between the living and after-living (the invisible ones), happens all the time. Its understanding has not been respectfully explored.

In this regard, I ponder this: "living knowing and knowable energy capable of emitting biophoton signals, and therein allow for our ability to speak to the invisible?" One such path in this exploration would be the African notion of "dreamtime walking." According to the Zulu shaman Credo Mutwa, to say "I dreamt" means "I flew" because there is something in the human that travels (walks) through time and can experience events before the physical body does. Both the Batonga and Zulu agree that if something is dreamed, it must be enacted. Once it is acted, the creative force of the soul that makes dreams recognizes this and brings you more dreams to guide you to make life more interesting. Africans spend a great deal of energy acting out dreams, which sometimes can have disastrous consequences, but Mutwa believes it is important to pay attention to them—those caused by indigestion aside—because they are a form of communication, no matter how silly they may seem. One way to tell if a dream carries a significant message is that it is in brilliant color, occurs just before dawn, or recurs two or three times during the night. Also, rubbing the back of the head on awakening can help with dream recollection or effacing, as in the case of nightmares. Herein, I would like to suggest that visitations from the departed may in fact be the experience of the living knowable and knowing spirit dreamtime walking with an after-living (the invisible ones) knowing and knowable Spirit.

NOSOLOGY AND CLASSIFICATION

Consistent with these ideas is the need for a Spirit classification of Dis-at-Ease. The most profound lingering psychological effects of slavery and colonialism for African people have been a sense of human alienation resulting from being infected with or assaulted by long-standing, ongoing sensorial information structures representing chattel enslavement and colonization, that is, the thingafication and dehumanization of African people. Human alienation for African people is the sense of being disconnected from one's Spirit (even though one is highly spiritual) and having a sense of not being truly or completely human (and not knowing it). This I have classified as "spirit damage" or the "suffering of the spirit." Consistent with these ideas are the need for a Spirit classification of Dis-at-Ease. Guided by the informative character of African deep thought, the development of an African-centered classification of disease, that is, nosology, should at minimum (a) use African language and logic and (b) explore the application and relevance of these ideas and notions in illuminating of the "suffering of the spirit." The "suffering of the spirit" can be evidenced in the experiences of being human—the expression of being human and the essence of being human itself. These three domains or paths represent the arenas of spirit suffering and imbalance or disharmony reflected in our shattered consciousness and fractured identity. The question to explore is how the violation, abandonment, or rejection of cultural precepts, themes, norms, and customs may serve as a source of Spirit Damage/Disconnect and "Tornadoes of the Mind" (mental illness).

The terminology and nomenclature must support a new nosology, classification of "disconnects" (disease), "spirit damage" (mental illness), and treatment (restoration) planning. In order to develop an authentic African-centered nosology, I would like to offer as a preliminary starting point the examination of the BaNtu notions of *Sumuna, Kingongo, Tunda Milongo, Kizongo Zongo, Nsumununu a Nkisa/Kinkongo* (Fu-kiau, 1991) and the Kemetic notion of *Serudja Ta. Sumuna* is the violation of self-sacredness. Inter-, intra-, and supra-relationships can violate the sacredness of self. *Tunda Milongi* is the violation of community laws and taboos which will lead to the condition of *Kizungu Zongo,* which represents mental chaos or tornadoes of the mind. The defiled or damaged Spirits (individual or collective) are seen as tornadoes of the mind or mental chaos. Both individuals and community as a whole can suffer from tornadoes of the mind. *Nsumununu* is when the Spirit of the community and the Spirit of its members become defiled or damaged. When a person or community does *Sumuna,* violates self-sacredness, the act or actions create *Nsumununu a Nkisa/Kinkongo*. In this circumstance, the individual or community has turned their backs on their own essence (sacredness in them), which is seen as Spirit defilement or insanity. Hence, it is suggested that what is considered mental illness or insanity in the African American community may, in fact, be spirit defilement or the "suffering of the spirit." Further elaboration of these African-centered classifications should consider how each of the above is expressed or exemplified and what predisposing factors and presenting problems (activities, actions, events, experiences, etc.) are associated with each of the above. It will be helpful to also know if there are triggers or stressors related to the onset of each of the above and what conditions support the continuation of the above conditions and impede their amelioration of the condition. In moving toward the task of restoration, it would also be important to imagine or determine what protective factors and restorative processes would be needed for each of the above.

Each of these notions or ideas should be vetted against the requirements that restorative relationships should represent spirit-grounded and charged relationships between healer and the healed, establish a binding commitment between the healer and healed to actively activate the restoration (healing) process, and reflect a conceptual schema or story that provides a culturally congruent explanation for the dis-at-ease and procedure or ritual for its resolution, including the recognition that the place or location for the healing is spirit driven and spirit filled.

In specific response to the shattering of African consciousness and the fracturing of Black identity (Nobles, 2007), I have proposed a recovery process called "reciprocal *srwd ta*" (re-birthing) of African spiritness. The idea of re-birthing requires a mutually interactive application of African wisdom traditions, history, culture, philosophy, and deep thought to illuminate, inform, and develop both the spiritness of (a) the person (personal character) and (b) the community (environmental character), by tapping into the most fundamental and essential core root and source for inspiring health and eliminating imbalance and discord and to reestablish or restore harmony and optimal human functioning. This by necessity will require an ongoing dialogue with traditional (not necessarily Western educated) *Nganga*, *Sangoma*, and so on.

Given the African American communal ethos and the importance of the collective, personhood existing within familyhood embedded in community should be the target or recipient of services. Operationally, personhood, familyhood, and neighborhood (community) can be seen as three interlinking rings or circles with wellness at their union point. Personhood existing within familyhood embedded in neighborhood should be the target or recipient of services. Operationally, personhood, familyhood, and neighborhood (community) serve as three integrated interlocking rings or circles with wellness as the union point. The locus of wellness is, therefore, the cojoining of participants including personhood, familyhood, neighborhood (peoplehood). The restoration of wellness should procedurally be designed to Mend the Essentiality (Spirit) and Connect the Nodal Disconnect (fractualization). The points, places, and portals wherein wellness (healing) occurs, emerges, and relates are at the intersect of personhood, familyhood, and neighborhood (peoplehood) via the combined and joint expressions and assistance of sound (drumming) and motion (dance), quieting (meditation), imagining, communing with nature, deep breathing, listening to (interviewing) and interacting with elders, and playing, especially with children.

EXISTENTIAL INTERLINKING OF PERSONHOOD, FAMILYHOOD, AND NEIGHBORHOOD

The existential interlinking of personhood, familyhood, and neighborhood should be the target or recipient of restoring wellness (healing services). Being under constant "psychic terrorism" indicates that all of us, all of the time, experience what is currently happening or has historically happened (threat, harm, disrespect, disregard, and destruction) to any Black person. This I have defined as Inter-Generational Sensori-Harm (IGSH). The psychic terrorism resulting from harm to any Black person causes all Black people to experience exacerbated, though subliminal, physical and psychological pain, trauma, and harm. Any and every act of violence, disregard, and disrespect can serve as hidden triggers for collective dis-at-ease and debilitating anger and dys- or misfunctioning.

As stated above, the requisite concepts are as follows: authenticity, African-centered learning inheres human *authenticity*. The idea of authenticity is larger than mere identity development as we commonly think of it. Authenticity means that one's identity is grounded in a collective ethnic and cultural consciousness; thus, the cultural resources of a community are the bases for both personal and collective identity. Authenticity best captures the intent of articulating a theory of human beingness that is centered in African realities. The clear identification of African ideals, images, and interests as codified in African worldviews and ideologies provides the only clear and consistent template for understanding African reality. Spiritness pertains to the condition of being spirit in totality. Spirit is the energy, force, or power that is both the inner essence and the outer envelope of human beingness. As energy, Spirit becomes *Spiritness* and therein serves to ignite and enliven the human state of being. It is both a metaphysical state and an ethereal extension or connection into and between the super world of the Deities, the interworld of other beings, and the inner world of the self.

ZOLA (LOVE) MAGNETIC ENERGY

ZOLA (love) (zoh-lah) is magnetic energy with an electrical charge that makes contact and connection between knowing and knowable Spirits (energy) to cause the activation of *Ngolo* (healing energy). *ZOLA* is the energy that causes the activation of molecular/cellular regeneration at both the material and immaterial levels. *Zaya* is the ability to imagine additional thoughts and ideas stimulated by the conversation (discussion or discourse). *Zaya* helps reveal what was lost or distorted, as well as "signposts" for reclaiming our way and restoring wellness going forward. Unlike the Western paradigm, life and living for the African is never experienced individually as an agent that is separate and distinct from all other individuals. Until imposed by the West, there was no such thing as an individual. The guiding principle for African people has been and remains the retention of a communal ethos that emphasizes the importance of the collective. (Be)ing is represented as within the existence of the family or tribe and experienced as personhood. What is misperceived and misunderstood as the individual is, in fact, personage or personhood as the special (and possibly unique) personal attributes, characteristics, and qualities of a particular manifestation of the communal or community (whole).

A person is a known, knowing, and knowable Spirit. Therefore, personhood theory is the study of the journey (development) of the known, knowing, and knowable human Spirit. Accordingly, it was noted (see Nobles, 2006, p. 1), that (1) a person, by law, is a being; (2) a person is spirit manifest; (3) a person has to *evolve* over the distance of being a being; (4) compassion dictates that a person cannot be thrown away; (5) a person is defined by uniqueness, relatedness, connection, and coherence; (6) a person is a person because there are other people; (7) a person is a being because of an indisputable connection between the person and God (belonging); (8) a person is able to say what and who one is and to define oneself as valuable (being); and (9) to become a being is the only important task of the person (becoming). Thus, to be human is to *belong* to Divine energy, to *be* inherently valued and valuable, and to be *becoming* perfectible.

The overall aim of personhood is to teach everyone the *essentiality* of the community for one's own survival or ascension and for the formation of one's identity as a person. We speak of *personhood* instead of personality to suggest the fullness of one's human expression that evolves over the arc of one's life. Thus, the whole of life is a process of learning to attain personhood and to be.

SIGNS AND THE SYMBOLIC

It is important to rescue the African consideration of signs and the symbolic. Signs and the symbols were used to represent the illumination or *Skh* via the synthesis of the visible and the invisible, the material and immaterial, the cognitive and emotive, the inner and the outer. The phenomenal world was illuminated (known) through speculative thought, which represented the subliminal and compensated for the inability to produce a sensation or a perception existing or functioning below the threshold of consciousness. The ancient technique of thinking depended upon a fuller and richer integration of the various manifestations of spirit, that is, so-called and mislabeled as mind, body, and spirit (Nobles, 2006, p. 102).

Ancient Egyptians educated the neurological structures of the brain so as to be able to maintain an active conscious connection between the bilateral lobes of the cerebral cortex and the impulses and subliminal information received from the more ancient and deeper brain centers. In doing so, the more ancient aspects of our nature were integrated into the activity of human reasoning and thought: cerebral cortex to limbic to R complex. Symbolism was a method used to illuminate, identify, and clarify the essential function or law of nature as, for example, embodied in the particular animal. Symbols were the objectification of things subjective in us and subliminal in nature. The activity of ancient human reasoning and thought was understood via an understanding of the symbolic method—Transformation-Synchronistic-Analogical (p. 101). The power of perceiving or comprehending was considered speculative thought which was more akin to intuitive if not visionary modes of apprehension. Speculative thought attempts to explain order and, above all else, unify experience for the knower.

African symbols and the symbolic developed over generations. Nodes of communication and meaning are layered on with each successive generation until whole aspects of cultural knowledge can be transmitted and translated through what I have termed memetic ideations. Throughout all of Africa (historically, contemporaneously, and both continental and diasporan), visual images, ordinary objects, and specific phrases are used symbolically to communicate knowledge, feelings, and values and to express, transmit, and store thoughts, emotions, and attitudes (Dzobo, 1992). Signs provide simple—as above, so below—symbols are used to convey "complex knowledge, abstract truths and ideas about life and its meaning" (p. 87).

The most straightforward example of a *sign* is the use of a *personal name*. The name is used as a sign and summons an appropriate action. But if the name is used in a conversation about that person, it would lead us to consider our perception of what the person bearing the name represents. Thus, the name is used as a *symbol*; it will not call forth actions appropriate to its subject but will make us think of its subject in certain ways. Thus, a symbol is a medium for conceiving a thing, enabling us to grasp the fullness of it. It invites mental images of the subject and constructs the subject within the contexts and subtexts of those mental images. The idea of a symbol consists in what it means as well as what it represents; it is a potent tool for bringing forth knowledge.

The use of signs and symbols provides the context for the reclamation and restoration of African-centered restorative language, where the terminology used becomes both signs and symbols for calling forth mental images and making us think of things in certain ways essential to the intent of African/Black psychology. This process of giving meaning to symbols is an oscillating synthesis between the person, the culture, and the symbols themselves. The potter, and not the pot, is responsible for the shape of the pot.

In a very real and concrete way, one must understand how the power embedded in symbols, thoughts, and ideas can invoke the energy (Spirit) within, create a state of enchantment, and open up a people's desire and ability to be well and whole.

SKH AND RESTORATIVE PRAXIS

African language and logic are the doorway into the new room of indigenous knowledge as praxis. As noted above, restoration or healing must involve the experience of being human, the expression of being human, and the essence of being human itself.

Accordingly, in this preliminary *Skh* exploration of Pan African humanness and the praxis of indigenous African knowledge systems, we conclude by inviting our colleagues to learn to recognize, respect, and appreciate the symbolic language and its representations; for example, the grandfather whose head developed into two heads which represent grandfathers of both the therapist and the client. As was noted above, *Sumunu* is caused directly by the breaking of taboos, cultural precepts, and ancestral traditions.

As practitioners of *Skh*, we have to appreciate the significance of exposing trainee therapists and psychologists to the African worldview, ontology, and culture, for example, *Ubuntu*, spiritual matters, living dead, performance of rituals, indigenous languages and meanings as core courses for psychologists of African descent working with African communities to avoid harming clients and to achieve epistemological justice. Hence, this discussion concludes by suggesting that in using African language and terminology, required by epistemic justice, when embraced, the ideas found in this discussion will offer unlimited opportunities to explore and address a whole unique, new, and original set of questions designed to illuminate the human spirit and treat and transform spirit damage at both the visible and invisible levels of reality. For example, the concepts and language of Western psychology prevent us from freely exploring the full (visible and invisible) reality of be(ing) African (whether continental or diasporan). Too often our exploration of African thought and behavior is conceptually incarcerated (Nobles, 1976) by the languages, concepts, and ideas that we have inherited from our Euro-American psychological education.

Parenthetically, this process can only be accomplished by interrogating the languages and logic of traditional African peoples, which, in turn, will allow greater insight into the functioning of contemporary African peoples. *Skh* operates from the basic premise that there is an African way of being that reflects an African "quality of thought and practice" (Nobles, 2015), rooted in the cultural images and interests of people of African ancestry (Karenga & Carruthers, 1986).

Unashamedly and unapologetically, give primacy to African languages, logic, terminology, and concepts (see Appendix 1: Critical Terms and Terminology), while providing theoretical guidelines and therapeutic applications and frameworks for healing programs and services. As a powerful example of the importance of language, note that the false separation between therapist and client (see Nobles et al., 2015) is dissolved by using African languages and referring to the person being treated as *bwana mboti,* or "the child of my ancestors" in Kikongo, and the therapist (also a Bwana Mboti) as an *nganga,* which means one who is capable of activating the process by which the person, family, or community repairs, cures, or restores itself to health and well-being. This small change in language dramatically changes the dynamic of the counseling session. The responsibility, dedication, and duty of mutually healing family is far greater and more important than the unidirectional working with a client. The importance of utilizing African languages and the ability to find correct meaning of terms and concepts is further hampered by our dependency on translations that were collected and crafted by mostly European missionaries. These translations were and should be suspect. In fact, we could apply the ancient adage, ascribe cultural etymology for methodological consistency *traduttore, traditor*, meaning "a translator is a traitor." We should understand this to mean that "treachery is in the translation." Note, for instance, in the *Dictionary and Grammar of the Kongo Language* (1887) the word *nganga* is translated as "a contentious fellow, or one who is always raising objections." An *Nganga* cures both physical and spiritual disease and serves as a powerful mediator between the visible world and the realm of Spirit and ancestors. They are capable of activating the process by which the body (persons or community) repairs, cures, or restores itself to health and well-being. The Kikongo word for shrine, *vela,* is translated to mean "heathen." The Yoruba word for a powerful woman is *iyami.* Yet it is translated as "witch." Parenthetically, it should also be noted that the word *witch* is derived from the Norwegian *vikja* and the Anglo-Saxon word *witega, wicca, wicce* (roughly meaning "to turn aside" and "to conjure away") and later through Christianity developed the meaning of a heathen devil worshipper. The total etymological history of this word is found in Europe, not Africa. Its application to the power of the feminine in Africa is indeed treasonous and misleading. Treachery and danger are embedded in the translation. Within imperial, colonial, and enslavement, beliefs and practices are deeply encoded ideations of African dehumanization expressed as the null or negation. These ideations serve constantly to replicate themselves and reinforce behaviors that sustain the ideation and therein deny or inhibit African people from having ideas of our own that counter this and are capable of creating new ideas or rescuing an indigenous African episteme upon which to draw.

Congruent with an African narrative and voice, African affirmation privileges the imagination that ought to fuel the investigation of African philosophy, literature, languages, history, politics, aesthetics, spirituality, and science, and encourages the interrogation of African essence, experience, and expressions, the nature of the beautiful, and the meaning of existence.

What is needed, however, is the binding language and logic that denotes Black excellence and allows and assists in the recognition and replication of the process.

Culture is the critical milieu without which human life cannot develop or exist. It is represented as the vast structure of behaviors, ideas, attitudes, values, habits, beliefs, customs, language, rituals, ceremonies, and practices "peculiar to a particular group of people and which provides them with a general design for living and patterns for interpreting reality." It is within this general design for living and patterning reality that the behaviors, beliefs, customs, and traditions take form as manifestations. It is the way in which everyday walkaround regular folks do and be. It is the milieu in which a people's social contract is fulfilled and the basic premise that reflects the African way of being. This paradigm shifting is not just an academic exercise in epistemic reflections. It has profound and real everyday implications and applications for everyday walkaround folks. In discussing the ideological configuration for civic commitment for African ancestry (both continental and diasporan) people, Asante and Ledbetter (2016) offer seven characteristics or features gleaned from successful historical African societies. They assert that, at the minimum, African social and civic engagements should have (1) an active and genuine promotion of African culture as determined by symbols motifs, rituals, education, scripts, proverbs, and ceremonies; (2) an emotional attachment to the subject from Africans and any social political economic agricultural literary or religious phenomenon that has implications for gender and class consideration; (3) active defense of African culture elements as historically valid in this context of art, music, education, science, and literature; (4) a celebration of centeredness and agency in an uncompromising commitment to the left that eliminates pejorative about Africans; (5) a powerful imperative for innovative research sources to revise the collective texts of African people; (6) massive acceptance of Africans as the nation that embraces diversity; and (7) an openness to include all of the elements and countries of African people as a collective gift of Africa to humanity (p. 78). Each of these becomes operational when cast as sociocultural behavioral and belief modalities that support, via *Skh*, wellness as having a profound sense of confidence, competence, and a sense of full possibility and unlimited potentiality.

RESTORATIVE PORTAL

As part of the African-centered paradigm shift, therapeutic practice or therapy is re-envisioned as a "restorative portal" through which one conjointly and across realms of reality goes through to access the activation of one's self-healing potential. As a portal, one is led to or through a pathway to the restoration of wellness. Any event or experience can serve as a restorative portal. Beauty parlors, barbershops, picnics, riding on the bus, playgrounds, working in the garden, drum circles, dance parties, or walking in the woods can all morph into restorative portals.

DISCONNECTS AS SPIRIT DAMAGE

We have proposed the following disconnects (see Nobles, 2022) as examples of our sense of Spiritness being damaged. They are (1) Self Disconnection: The idea that an individual could be in disharmony with their own personhood emanates from the complexity and multiplicity of the person in Ancient Kemetic/Bantu thought. The human person comprises multiple components, such as the physical body (*khat, umzimba*) that is liable to decay; the heart (*inhliziyo*), which is the source of good and evil thoughts; an abstract personality or individuality. Individual disharmony and illness could result from the imbalance between the various components (e.g., *Ba, Atmu, Seb*) of the self. Self-hatred, such as the desire to be or act as White, something that one is not, is another aspect of this internal disequilibrium; (2) Interpersonal Disconnection: This occurs when one fails to live in harmony with other people and their neighbors (*omakhelwane*). Violation of other human beings, through acts such as violence or rape, results from the failure to see the other human being as an integral aspect of the self and hence that violence or harm to the other is equivalent to self-harm. This is because all people exist as one in Spirit. Philosophical maxims such as *umuntu ngumuntu ngabantu* (it is in recognizing others as human and acting on those bases, that one becomes fully human) and *motho ubebelwa munwe* (a person is born for the other) *all* point toward human interdependence as an indispensable aspect of Be-ing. Racial hatred, gender-based violence, and violence against infants and elderly

The Re-harmonization (Therapeutic) Portal

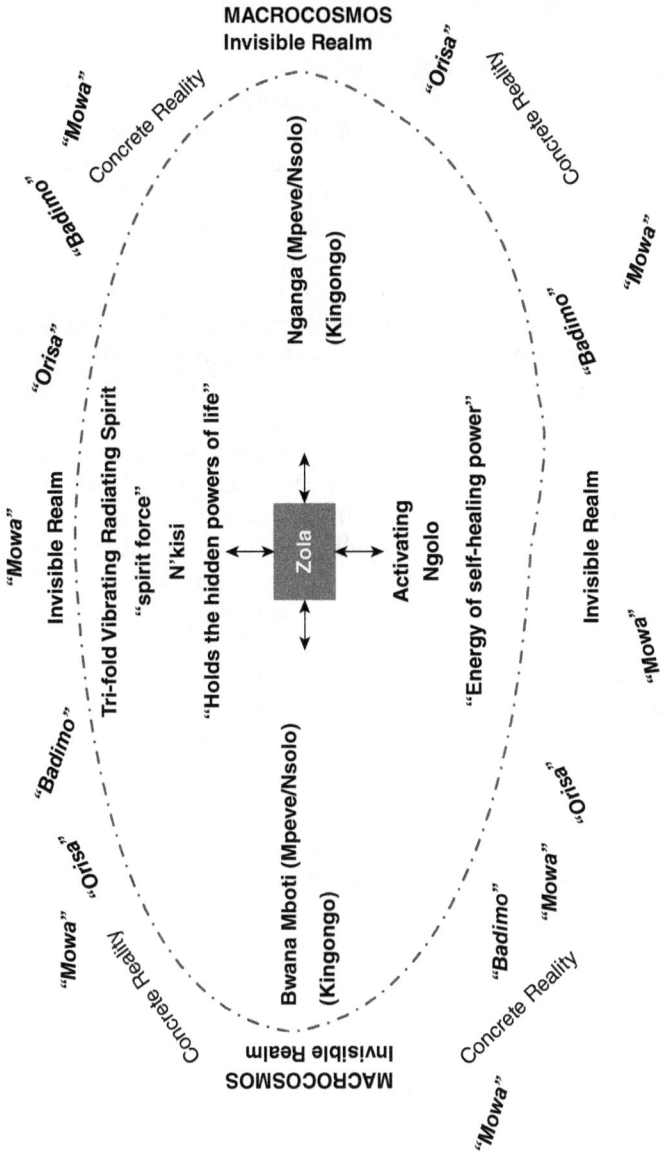

MACROCOSMOS
Invisible Realm

"Orisa"

Concrete Reality

"Mowa"

"Badimo"

"Mowa"

Nganga (Mpeve/Nsolo)
(Kingongo)

"Badimo"

"Orisa"

Invisible Realm

"Mowa"

Tri-fold Vibrating Radiating Spirit
"spirit force"
N'kisi

"Holds the hidden powers of life"

Zola

Activating
Ngolo

"Energy of self-healing power"

Invisible Realm

"Mowa"

"Badimo"

Bwana Mboti (Mpeve/Nsolo)
(Kingongo)

"Orisa"

"Mowa"

"Orisa"

"Mowa"

Concrete Reality

"Badimo"

"Mowa"

MACROCOSMOS
Invisible Realm

Concrete Reality

"Mowa"

93

people all stem from the ignorance of our mutual Spiritness; (3) Family and Ancestral Lineage Disconnection: This may come about as a result of a range of factors, including the failure to honor one's ancestors, while religiously honoring the ancestors of one's oppressors. In indigenous African epistemology, it is understood that the ancestors withdraw their protection from the family if the elders fail to perform appropriate libations. The withdrawal of protection manifests in the form of misfortune or illness (symptoms), which are compounded until there is an appropriate diagnosis and the problem is addressed; (4) Historical and Linguistic Disconnection: This refers to the loss of historical memory, which is essential in defining the community as a people with artistic and scientific achievements. It also includes the loss of the right to name oneself and the landscape, and the tendency to belittle African languages in favor of European languages, leading ultimately to linguicide; (5) Epistemological Disconnection: This refers to disconnection from indigenous knowledge bases, philosophies, and value systems and practices. Just as there is an aftereffect (post-harm or trauma) when persons are victimized by crime or assault, there is an unaddressed harm or illness associated with epistemicide and menticide. This is particularly due to the schooling systems' unwillingness to connect with the multiple ecologies of knowledge, instead openly championing Western knowledge systems as being superior to other knowledge systems, albeit in the absence of compelling evidence to this effect; (6) Ecological Disconnection: African knowledge systems propose a holonic (fractalized) universe in which human beings are part and parcel and reflective of their surrounding ecological environment; (7) Material Disconnection: This refers to the loss of personal and collective dignity due to poverty, loss, and ultimately, dehumanization; (8) Disconnection from the Land: This refers to indigenous people's loss of land and displacement, leading to the loss of a livelihood and inability to perform critical self-defining rituals such as the right to bury and continue to honor the deceased.

The existential interlinking of personhood, familyhood, and neighborhood should be the target or recipient of restoring wellness (healing services).

INTERCONNECTING RINGS

Unlike the Western paradigm, life and living for the African is never experienced "individually" as an agent that is separate and distinct from all other individuals. Until imposed by the West, there was no such thing as an individual. The guiding principle for African people has been and remains the retention of a communal ethos that emphasizes the importance of the collective. (Be)ing is represented as within the existence of the family or tribe and experienced as "personhood." What is misperceived and misunderstood as the individual is, in fact, personhood as the special (and possibly unique) personal attributes, characteristics, and qualities of a particular manifestation of the communal (whole).

Interconnecting Rings of Wellness

Personhood

Wellness

Familyhood   Neighborhood

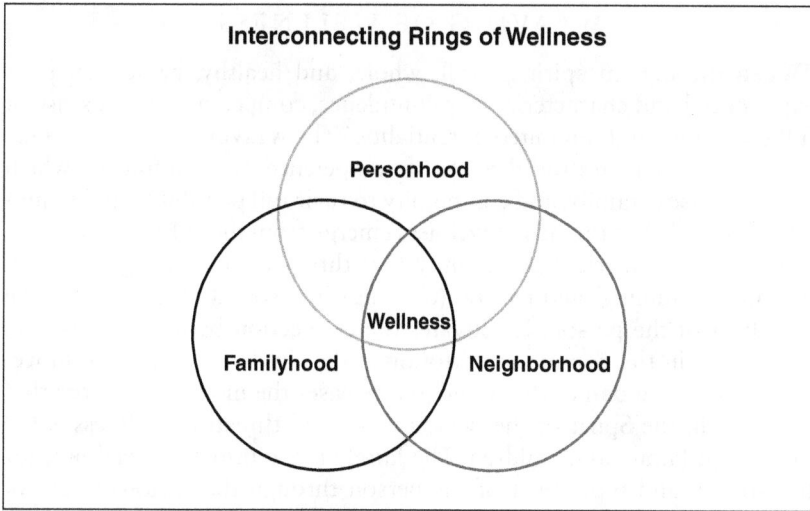

This fundamental paradigm shift with the Interconnecting Rings of Wellness becomes (see figure above) the collaborative spiraling work that allows the clinician and client to flow from shifting the paradigm to internalizing essential new meanings to obtain an enduring understanding of what it means to be a Spirit being—to boldly engage in *Zaya* discourse leading to the co-creation of the restoration of wellness.

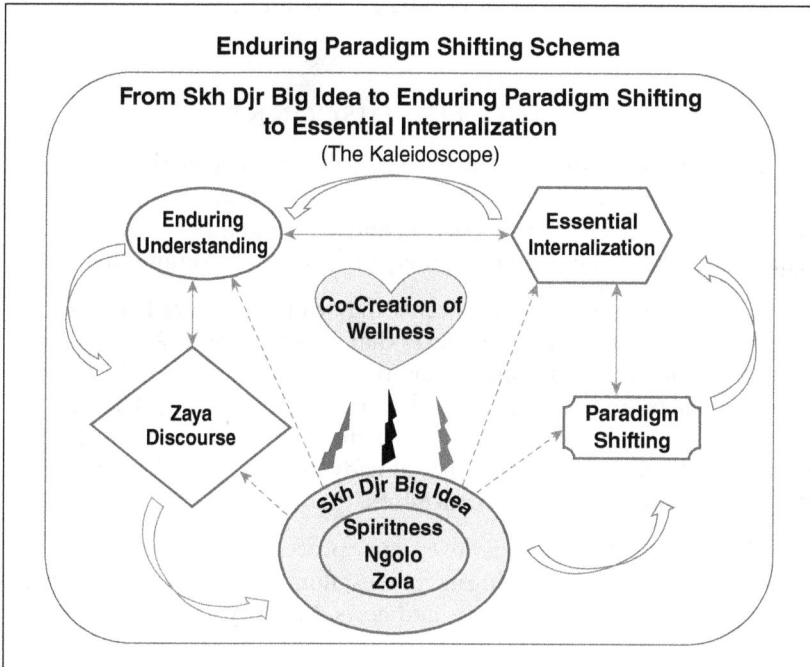

Enduring Paradigm Shifting Schema

From Skh Djr Big Idea to Enduring Paradigm Shifting to Essential Internalization
(The Kaleidoscope)

Enduring Understanding

Essential Internalization

Co-Creation of Wellness

Zaya Discourse

Paradigm Shifting

Skh Djr Big Idea
Spiritness
Ngolo
Zola

WEAVING OF WELLNESS

"When the human spirit is well, whole, and healthy, being human is experienced and characterized by confidence, competence, and a sense of full possibility and unlimited potentiality." The weaving of wellness must identify and activate the threads of competence and confidence which link the person, family, and community to their full possibility and unlimited potential. The threads of wellness emerge from the cultural substance of the African American community. One thread is sound (singing, chanting, and drumming) and motion (dancing). The sound of the drum is the heartbeat of the person. It activates the connection between the person and others in the community. Motion is the rhythmic pattern of movement that accompanies the sound and releases the molecular energy that is at rest in the Spirit of the person. A second thread of wellness is the sanctity of family and children. The family is the primary social unit for the growth and movement of the person through the various stages of Being, Becoming, Belonging, and ultimately actualizing their personhood. Another thread is the power of the word, *Nommo*, to cause the thing to come into being. The final thread is the use of rituals. A ritual is a prescribed form or method for the performance of an important event or special behavior. The doing or performance of rituals reminds the participant of who they are and that they are part of something greater than their individual selves. Ritual performance reveals the deeper and more profound purpose in life while reinforcing right conduct and the more noble aspects of being human. These are some of the major threads that are woven into the tapestry of healing and wellness.

MENDING THE DISCONNECT

The restoration of virtue and character is the ultimate goal and purpose of "mending the disconnects" wherein one strives to produce a person who is whole, honest, just, respectful, and skilled and the cause and consequence of the social wellness (order) of family and community.

The mending of the discontent technology can be achieved through the use of five restorative "RE" processes that are intentional. A central component of our African-centered approach is a healing and revealing process. Practitioners are grounded in the understanding that our primary task is to help our people reconnect with their core spiritual identity and African humanity that already exists within them and links them across time and place to ancestors.

RE-Memorying: Healing involves the process of "rememorying"—reconstructing our stories (Spirits, bodies, families, and "psyches") from the fragments of memory, gossip, and news. Memory and storytelling are reconnective processes that can help us live more harmoniously with ourselves, family, community, and the past (Akinyela, 2005).

RE-Alignment: Reconnecting a sense of personhood—spiritual, communal, cultural (physical/environmental), and personal potentials (Grills & Rowe, 1996)—is a second healing aim with African people.

RE-Building: Rebuilding refers to developing sociocommunal systems that replicate and reproduce African notions of human beingness, features of human functioning, and optimal human development. Rebuilding fractured Spirits requires collective, communal, and specific cultural practices; it is impossible to address symptoms of disorder by imposing or reinforcing isolation to reinstitute order within the person.

RE-Vitalization: Grounded in the importance of spiritual experience for mending the disconnect, the healing aim of revitalization focuses on helping persons to see themselves as Spirit manifestation. Ongoing healing becomes the process and state of guiding and developing the person's ability to experience the extraordinary, special, and divine Spirit within (Nobles et al., 1995).

RE-Storation: Restoration represents revival through strengthening interdependence and communal connectivity, fostering a sense that life unfolds in intimate reciprocity and regains the capacity to experience life with a fullness of belonging, being, and becoming.

Indigenous healing is defined as "helping beliefs and strategies that originate within a culture or society and that are designed for treating the members of a given cultural group" (Constantine et al., 2004, p. 111). For people of African ancestry, indigenous healing includes values, beliefs, and a worldview that recognizes a connection between mind, body, and spirit (Obasi et al., 2009). These domains of mind, body, and spirit are incorrect. For African people everything is Spirit. There is only Spirit that manifests as mind and body. As default, African American practitioners have adopted the Western domains and defined mental health problems according to these three domains. Culturally congruent (African-centered) intervention strategies should incorporate orality as material and immaterial manifestations of Spirit; divination as the utilization of spirit techniques; and healing beliefs originating from and designed to specifically treat African American people. Such interventions incorporate culturally congruent practices that are reflective of the worldview of African people (Ojelade et al., 2014, p. 493). By definition, the science of African human functioning, ergo, *Skh* is the intellectual activity encompassing the systematic study, understanding, knowing, and illumination of African Being, and technology is the practical application of scientific knowledge.

Skh ultimately requires our direct engagement with the invisible realm. This extended contact between and within the invisible realm is an area of knowing and being that our materialist-based episteme and knowing framework has not prepared us to scientifically honor. Probably, with the limited exception of dreaming, we have only had brief informal exploration of extended contact (visitations) and communication with the "invisible ones" (deceased). Clearly there is a new frontier of knowing to be explored.

ENDNOTES

1. Without much debate, the history of mainstream (modern) Western philoso-phy and its application to social inquiry (social behavioral sciences) has been influenced by many great Western thinkers but none as more foundational than Aristotle 1 (384 BCE–322 BCE) and Descartes (1596–1650). I, therefore, must begin this discussion by first addressing the spell of Aristotle and Descartes on modern analyses and critique. Starting with the Greek philoso-phers, the Aristotelian/Descartian spell has become the curse of "dualism" (truth vs. falsity, good vs. evil, fate vs. freewill, one vs. many, chaos vs. order, simplicity vs. complexity, matter vs. energy, thesis vs. antithesis, positivism vs. idealism, wave vs. particle, mind vs. body, space vs. time, behaviorism vs. vitalism, etc.) which has haunted both the episteme and method of scientific knowing and understanding, especially "Descartes dilemma" of the mind vs. the body. Breaking away from the Greek Ghost of Western Intellectual thought, especially as Descartes Dilemma, is critical to the following explora-tion of ancestral consciousness and communicating with the Invisible Ones.

2. The range of meaning of *Dar* includes "search out, investigate, seek, probe, plan, and take thought for the future" (Faulkner 1976, pp. 176, 320). The ancient Egyptian word *djaer* has its origin in medical terminology and means to probe deeply and widely in examination; here, by extension, a profound and prolonged probing into oneself in order to understand and assert oneself in the most dignity-affirming and expansive ways. Skh Djr was previously used to represent engaging in a deep, profound, and pene-trating search, study, understanding, and mastery of the process of illuminating the human spirit, and the Skh investigatory method required the illumination of the invisible in order to achieve "transformative-synchronistic-analogic" insight and modality. The Skh task of "uncovering" is to illuminate (identify and clarify) the hidden essential function or law of nature in order to fully understand the phenomena of being. Every recogniz-able element in nature is a "symbol" representing an essential function or law. In this text I use *Skh* as the overarching title for the Science of Being.

3. Africans on the continent and throughout the diaspora are fundamentally BaNtu people. In fact, it is only in understanding the BaNtu-Kongo ideas and meanings of being human that one will be able to better or more fully determine the impact of the Trans-Saharan and Transatlantic slave trade.

4. Spiritness is the essence of being and recognizes being as being in the visible (material) reality as simply a manifestation of the invisible. Hence as a Spirit being, so-called human beings are living suns, possessing a "knowing and knowable" Spirit (energy or power) through which there is an enduring relationship with the total perceptible and ponderable universe.

5. "Sensorial information structures" that are contagious information patterns that reproduce by symbiotically infecting human minds and altering their behavior, causing them to propagate certain patterns of behavior. Functionally, memes are any contagious information patterns, in the form of symbols, sounds, and/or movement, that are capable of being perceived by any of the senses and replicated by symbiotically entering the human being's "mind" and thus altering behavior in a way that propagates itself.

6. Music, as rhythmic sound, changes our heartrates, breathing, and blood pressure, and alters our heart rate variability, indicators of cardiac and mental health. Neuroscientists have traced music-induced physiological changes to a central node in the brain's networks, called the anterior insular, with dense connections to the vagus nerve, responsible for unconscious regulation of body functions.

7. For a further discussion of sensorial informational ideations, see Shattered Consciousness, Fractured Identity: Black Psychology and the Restoration of the African Psyche, *Journal of Black Psychology* 2013, *39*(3), 232–242.

8. See Dr. Charles Finch's provocative and illuminating discussion of quantum consciousness as the fifth dimension in his book *The Star of Deep Beginnings: The Genesis of African Science and Technology*.

9. Quantum particles seem to affect each other instantaneously even if they are far away from each other (Einstein's spooky behavior at a distance).

10. The ancient Kemites believed that all phenomena emerged from *Nu*, the primordial substance. The person, it was believed, also evolved from *Nu*, the primordial substance. Ancient Kemetic mythology suggests that *Nu* manifested itself as a "person" so that it could "appear" in "glory" on earth. The ancient Kemetic definition of the human being emphasized, at minimum, the consubstantiality of the primordial substance (and phenomenal expressions); the primacy of the person; perpetual evolution (perfectibility) and eternal life. The character of the person was continually challenged in response to the challenge of one's destiny. For the Kemites the challenge was, through perfecting, to live throughout the millennia, to be forever "noble," to be "the princes of eternity." In ancient Kemet, it was also understood that *Sahu* travels within, between, and throughout all forms of existence. It is nonmaterial. As *Khat*, it gives power to the spiritual and mental realms. As *Akhu* which is in the blood, it radiates or shines throughout the *Khu* (1st soul or divine intelligence) and the *Ab* which is the seat of wisdom, knowledge, and understanding which links the physical body with spiritual body. Represented as the *Ba* (resides in the *ab*) it takes on human form and can be material or not depending on its own will. The *Sahu* has eternal and unchanging knowledge—can fly like bird, leave the body at

sleep, and return. It represents consciousness and time as the rhythm of experience. *Ka–* is associated with emotional body. The *Ka* is an abstract personality capable of assuming form without matter and resembling the person it inhabits. Related to spiritual being, it gives rise to movement. The *Khasbut* is the shadow. It is capable of existing outside of the body connected to the person; if the shadow is captured, the person could literally die; it may be associated with dreams, hallucinations, and ordinary vision. The *Khat* is the physical body; it corrupts after death. Animated by the *Ba*, it regulates or is associated with awareness of bodily functions, elimination, autonomic functioning, unconscious breathing, heartbeat, etc. The *Sekhem* is the vital power which allows beings to become incarnate. It travels between life and death. It is the power/energy which allows reincarnation. The *Ren* resides in a person's name. To blot a person's name from history is to banish them to oblivion.

11.   Mbiti says that Africans have two periods of time, **The Sasa** (actual time) events occurring in the present are in the past and **The Zamani** (potential time) events pertaining to rhythm of nature which extend into the immediate future, e.g., pregnancy and changing seasons constitute potential time. As noetic sensoria, the Akan conception of the nature of being human also informs the concept of the person. The Akan people consider a human being to be comprised of three elements. The first element is the *Okra,* which constitutes the innermost self, the essence of the person (Gyekye, 1987, p. 9). The *Okra* is considered the living soul of the person and is sometimes referred to as the *Okrateasafo.* As the living soul, the *Okra* is identical with life. It is also the embodiment and transmitter of the individual's *Nkrabea* (destiny). As the life force, the *Okra* is linked to *Honhom* (breath) (1987, p. 95). The *Honam,* however, is the tangible and recognizable manifestation of the presence of the *Okra.* The second element of the person is the *Sunsum.* The term *Sunsum* is used to refer to all unperceivable, mystical beings, and forces. It is the activating principle in the person (1987, p. 88). The *Sunsum* is what molds the child's personality and disposition. It is that which determines the character. The *Okra,* in turn, manifests itself in the world of experience through the *Sunsum.* The final component is simply the *Honam* (the body), which is made up of *Ntoro* and *Mogya* (1987). While the *Okra* and the *Sunsum* come from *Onyame* (God), the *Ntoro* and the *Mogya* are derived from other humans, i.e., one's parents. In their conception of the nature of the person, the Akan believe that the *Ntoro* is derived from the father's sperm and the *Mogya* is derived from the mother's blood. The *Okra* and the *Sunsum* constitute a spiritual unity. Hence, the person is made up of two principal components, the immaterial/spiritual (*Okra & Sunsum*) and the material/physical (*Honam*). In terms of the relation between the soul and the body, Akan thinkers contend that not only does the body influence the soul, the soul also influences the body. The Akan believe that the relation between the soul (*Okra and Sunsum*) and the body (*Honam*) is so close that they comprise an indissoluble and indivisible unity. Hence, the person is a homogeneous entity or value.

12.   As noetic sensoria, the Yoruba believe that the person is made up of a spirit and a body (Opoku, 1978, p. 92). The body or *Ara* is formed by the divinity,

Orisha-nla. It is through the *Ara* that man responds to his environment. It is the part of the person which can be touched and felt. It can be damaged and disintegrates after death. The spirit component of the person is the *Emi* (spirit). The *Emi* gives life to the person. The *Emi* is the divine element of the person and links the person directly to God. Upon the death of the person, the *Emi* returns to *Elemi* (the owner of the spirit, God) and continues to live. As a person, one also possesses an inner head or *Ori Inu.* The *Ori Inu* is given directly by *Oludumare.* It is the person's personal spirit. The *Ori Inu* is the guardian of the self and the carrier of one's destiny. It also influences the personality of the person. In addition to the *Emi* and the *Ori Inu,* the person has an *Okan* (1978, p. 93). The word *Okan* means heart, but as a constituent component of the person, it represents the immaterial element that is the seat of intelligence, thought, and action. Hence, it is sometimes referred to as the "heart-soul" of the person. The *Okan* is believed to exist even before the person's birth. It is the *Okan* of the ancestors which is reincarnated in the newborn child. To be a person, the Yoruba also believe that one must have *Ori* and *Eje.* The *Ori* rules, controls, and guides the person's life and actually activates the person. The *Ori* is the bearer of one's destiny and helps the person to fulfill what they came to earth to do. The *Ori* is simultaneously the "essence of the person" and the person's "guardian and protector" (1978, p. 93). The *Ori* is closely associated with the *Emi.* The *Eje* is the blood. It is the physical expression of an electro-chemical/magnetic energy that is the force which binds and animates life. The Yoruba also believe that the *Iye* is a component of the person. The *Iye* is the immaterial element that is sometimes referred to as the mind (1978, p. 93). The person also has *Ojiji* (shadow). The *Ojiji* is a constant companion throughout one's life and ceases to exist when the *Ara* (body) dies.

13. As noetic sensoria, the Sonay people of Mali, the word for black is *bibi* (Maiga, 1996, p. 17). *Bibi* is actually a concept used to refer to the essential goodness of things. It is never used to refer to anything negative or inferior. The full significance of this concept is found in the expression *wayne bibi* (black sun). Dr. Hassimi Maiga (1996, p. 18) notes that the Gao people of Mali use the term *wayne bibi* to refer to the hottest part of the day when the sun is at its fullest. In effect, *wayne bibi* refers to the fullest expression of the sun. It is when the sun is the brightest, the most dazzling, and the most radiant. The black sun *(wayne bibi)* symbolizes "luminosity," the state of being unlimited and the condition that when a thing achieves its total expression. Similarly, the Sonay people use the term *Ay moo hari bibi* (Give me black water) to signify water that is from the deepest part of the river and the most clear and clean (p. 18). *Bibi* in this context represents the depth or essence, clarity and purity of a thing. Hence, the term *bibi,* especially *wayne bibi,* connotes a state wherein a thing is pure, clean, clear, limitless, luminous, radiant, and exuding its totality or fullest expression. Accordingly, I am suggesting that the Sonay term *wayne bibi* be used to represent the notion of Spiritness in human beings. In the state of being a Spirit, and in recognition of the idea that the birth of a human being symbolizes the rising of a living sun in the upper world, the Spiritness or *wayne bibi* (black sun) of our being represents the unlimited radiance, luminosity,

and dazzle, and total expression of being human. It is believe that when the person or community experience congruity between the supra-, inter-, and inner realms of the *wayne bibi* (Spiritness), then the sense of human integrity is achieved. This is a critical formulation because, I believe, that for African people, particularly those who were colonized and enslaved, it is only when one has a sense of the "Black Sun," the *wayne bibi* that one has the "instinct" to resist dehumanization or oppression as well as the capability to even contemplate human liberation and potential. It is also the awakening of the *wayne bibi* that allows us to contemplate and believe in the certainty of victory and human possibility. At the metaphysical level, the *wayne bibi,* therefore, is the unlimited and total expression of energy and power that represents human possibility, probability, and potential. At the physical level, the *wayne bibi* is experienced as a drive or human condition. *Wayne bibi* (black sun) is experienced as an urge and desire for what is excellent, good, and right. As the fullest expression of goodness, it eventuates in the ever-expanding love and feeling of good will for all life. It is the *wayne bibi* that makes for ethical character and proper conduct. Being the Black Sun, the *wayne bibi,* the person has an ever-present urge to kindness, goodwill, and fellowship. This is often experienced as the "felt need" to love and be loved for no particular reason at all. The *wayne bibi* gives the person the desire for order and the beautiful, i.e., that which is essential, pure, clean, clear, radiant. It is the *wayne bibi* that serves as the impetus for concern beyond self to other and the emotional "sense of the Divine agency" and relationship in human affairs (i.e., the compelling need to understand the nature of the Divine) and thereby life itself and our meaning and purpose in life. The human being as a living sun expresses one's humanity as the magnetic pull away from mere animal or physical existence and toward that which is higher, nobler, better, and more excellent (The Godness/Goodness). It is the *wayne bibi,* the Black Sun, the unlimited luminosity, the radiance, the totality or fullest expression of Divine energy that gives one the sense of inner power and dignity and makes one human. The notion of being a power (*wayne bibi*) of perpetual veneration suggests precise meanings for the concepts of being, becoming, and belonging found in the African centered discourse. "Being" is the state of *wayne bibi,* i.e., having the quality of a living sun. It is to have an essence or substance that is an attribute of the Divine and is absolutely invariant and indestructible. "Becoming" is to fulfill one's destiny. It is the continuous and constant (movement toward) achievement or realization of potential(s) to reach higher levels of actuality. "Belonging" is the condition wherein one is conscious of the state of being one with that which is whole. It is a condition wherein one is integrally and essentially infused or blended with that which is greater.

14. As noetic sensoria, the Mende believed the person to be made up of the *Ngafa* (the Spirit) and the *Nduwai* (the flesh) (1979, p. 94). The *Ngafa* is immaterial and is provided by the mother. It leaves the body at death and goes into the land of the spirits. The *Ngafa* is the psychic constituent of the person. The *Nduwai* is the physical part of the person and is provided by the father. The *Nduwai* is, in part, contained in the seminal fluid. The

"shadow" (*Nenei*) is also part of the person (Harris & Sawyer, 1968, p. 88) and is believed to report the death of the body to God. The Mende believe that a healthy Spirit (*Ngatha*) produces a state of *Guhun* (total well-being). The person's name is closely associated with his *Ngafa*. The significance of the name is that the Mende believe that a person's *Ngafa* can travel from the person during sleep or other state of unconsciousness. However, a person can be revived or awakened when one's name is called repeatedly. The Mende, therefore, believe that the person's name may be the component that wakes up the *Ngafa* or the human Spirit.

15. The Zulu speaking people of South Africa, like almost all African people, have an ancient text, the *Izaga*, in which they define the meaning of what it is to be a person (Ngubane, 1979, p. 60). The text of "wise" sayings contain the Zulu interpretation of the teachings of the Sudic philosophy. Within these teachings, the Zulu say *"Umuntu Ngumuntu,"* meaning, "the person is human." In this same regard, Dr. Marimba Ani teaches that the Bantu belief about the concept of the person is crystallized in the saying *Umuntu Ngu Muntu Nga Bantu,* which means "A person is a person because there are people." In believing that the primordial substance was infinite, the Zulu believe that all phenomena was made of the primordial substance. The person was one such phenomenon. The ancient Zulu philosophers taught, in this regard, that through the *Umuntu Ngumuntu,* the human person was unique in that the person defined oneself and is essentially knowledgeable of one's own intrinsic value. For the Zulu to be human is to be able to say what and who one is and to be able to define oneself as a value. Ngubane (1979, p. 62) argues that the African understanding of the person is a "protein" evaluation of the human being which flowed into Nile Valley high culture of the Ancient Kemites and subsequently created clusters of similar conceptions all over Africa. What, in fact, is recognized as African culture and civilization is the combined social conventions and inventions emerging from a common African meaning of the person. Like the Kemites, the Zulu believed that all phenomena (*Uluthu*) had their origins in a "living consciousness" (1976), which they called *UQOBU*. The person evolved from the *UQOBU* in response to *Umthetho weMvelo* (the law of appearing), the demands of *Isimu* (one's nature), and *Ukuma Njalu* (perpetual evolution). According to Ngubane (p. 77) the central teaching of the Buntu is that all things originated from *UQOBU* and evolve in response to the challenge of their nature. The person, according to the Zulu, is a self-defining value and that life's purpose for the person is perpetual evolution. The Zulu ideal emphasized the primacy of the person and the creation of a society which equipped, enabled, and ensured that the person would realize the promise of being or becoming human (*Ukuba Ngumuntu*) (p. 77). As a person, the components of realizing the promise of being human are (a) the person by law is human (*Umuntu Ngumuntu*), (b) the person has to evolve over the distance of being human (*Amabanga Okuba Ngumuntu*), and (c) human compassion dictates that the person can not be "thrown" away (*Ukuba Ngumuntu*) (p. 93).

16. The BaNtu-Kongo believe that the heated force of Kalunga blew up and down as a huge storm of projectiles, *kimbwandende,* fusing together a huge

mass. In the process of cooling, solidification of the fused mass occurs, giving birth to the Earth (Fu-Kiau, 2001). In effect, the BaNtu believe that all of reality (*kalunga*) is fundamentally a process of perpetual and mutual sending and receiving of Spirit (energy) in the form of waves and radiations. *Kalunga* or reality is the totality, the completeness of all life. It is an ocean of energy, a force in motion. *Kalunga* is everything, sharing life and becoming life continually after life itself. As the totality or the complete living, *kalunga* is comprised of both a visible realm (*ku nseke*) and an invisible realm (*ku mpemba*). The visible physical world has Spirit (energy) as its most important element or nature. Referred to as *nkisi* (medicine), the spirit element of the physical (visible) world has the power to care, cure, heal, and guide. The invisible (spiritual) world (*ku mpemba*) is comprised of human experience, ancestor experience, and the soul-mind experience. The *ku mpemba* has Spirit (energy) as its most important element or nature. In effect, if reality (visible and invisible) is, it is Spirit. All that exist are, therefore, different concrete expressions of Spirit. In effect, Being is being spirit in a reality of Spirit. Fu-Kiau (2001) further clarifies that the human being or *muntu* is a "threefold unfolding" experience in the realms of yet-to live, living, and after living. He further notes that a human being is a living sun (energy), possessing "knowing and knowable" Spirit (energy) through which Spirit in human form has an enduring relationship with the total perceptible and ponderable universe. The BaNtu-Kongo believe that diverse forces and waves of energy that govern life surround humans. This fire-force called *kalunga* is complete in and of itself and emerges within the emptiness or nothingness and becomes the source of life on earth. *Ubuntu:* In terms of *ubuntu*, the construct *ntu* is thought to be the universal expression of Spirit or force. *Ntu* inseparable from *umu* is Being itself (Kagame, 1989). Conceptually, *ntu* as a modal point at which Spirit as being assumes concrete form, is reflected in four categories of expression in BaNtu philosophy. In effect, there is one essence with four categories of expression. Human beings (*Mu Ntu* or *Muntu*) are an expression of Spirit or force (*Ntu*). Place and Time (*Ha Ntu* or *Hantu*) are equally expressions of Spirit or force (*Ntu*). All the material objects (*Ku Ntu* or *Kuntu*) are equally spirit expressions (*Ntu*). *Ubuntu* is, therefore, Spirit in which Being and beings coalesce. It is the cosmic universal force. Being human is to be Spirit, energy or power. Being Spirit is to be one who lives and moves within and is inseparable from the ocean of waves and radiations of Spirit (energy or power). A human being is Spirit who affirms one's humanity by recognising the humanity of others and on that basis establishes humane relations with them. A human being is Spirit whose unfolding is a constant and continual inquiry into its own being, experience, knowledge, and truth (Ramose, 1991). To be human is to be a Spirit in motion (unfolding). Being human is being a phenomenon of perpetual, constant, and continual unfolding (vibration—sharing and exchanging) of life spirit. Humans are containers and instruments of Divine spirit and relationships. A human being is akin to a living sun (unlimited power), possessing a "knowing and knowable" Spirit (energy or power) through which one has an enduring relationship with the total perceptible and ponderable universe. The human being is a threefold unfolding experience of yet-to-live, living, and after-living Spirit. The BaNtu concepts of Spirit are these: (1) *Muntu*: *Muntu* includes the living and the dead, orishas, loas, and Bon Dieu [the good Lord]. *Muntu* is therefore a force endowed with intelligence. *Muntu* is an entity which is a force which has control over *Nommo*; (2) *Kintu*: *Kintu* embraces those forces which cannot act for themselves and which can become active only on the command of a *Muntu*. . . . In the category *Kintu* belong plants, animals, minerals, tools, objects of customary usage, and so on; (3) *Hantu*: Space and time fall together in the category *Hantu*; and, (4) *Kuntu*: includes forces such as beauty and laughing. *Nommo*, the magic power of the word: "*Nommo;* the power of the word is the physical-spiritual life force which awakens all sleeping forces and gives physical and spiritual life." What sets the highest beings apart is that they are beings that have control of language, and through language, they are able to control other beings. Ultimately, the BaNtu-Kongo people believe that the person is an energy, Spirit, or power. And as a Spirit, the person is a phenomenon of "perpetual veneration." The person is both the container and instrument of Divine energy and relationships. Consistent with the Mali notion *wayne bibi,* noetic sensoria would conceive of being and consciousness as being a living (black) sun, possessing a "knowing and knowable" Spirit (energy) through which one has an enduring relationship with the total perceptible and ponderable universe.

17. Black Identity is a designation given to a group of people having highly melanated (dark) skin. However, consistent with the Western Grand Narrative, black represents the opposite of white and connotated all that was bad, wicked, evil, and dangerous. Black people (the cursed of Ham) were (are) evil, bad, undeserving of respect or regard and should be feared, controlled, exploited, eliminated, dominated/destroyed.

VI

Culture as Restorative Technology

A priori Certainty: *"All is spirit. If it exists, it most assuredly is spirit."*

In addressing the question of what is culture, McNair (2004) prefaces his exhaustive review by noting that *"the human spirit evolves through a variety of different groups and subgroups through the medium of culture. It therefore needs a variety of different cultural experiences to realize its full potential or to fulfill itself. Every human culture is a fairly unique expression of the human spirit."* In referencing the symbolic anthropologist Clifford Geertz (1973) he further acknowledges culture as *historically transmitted patterns of meanings embodied in symbols, a system of inherited conceptions expressed in symbolic forms by means of which men, errata people, communicate, perpetuate and develop their knowledge about their attitudes toward life* (Geertz 1973, p. 89). McNair notes that Ani (1994) and my own work (Nobles, 1985) define culture in a way that includes and requires the idea of spirit. Additionally, as discussed below, I also have positioned spirit as fundamental to African ancestry people's culture and the key to culture having its restorative feature or property.

In transitioning to the restorative technology that merges with the science of Being, we believe it's informative to revisit the issue of culture as technology. Culture as restorative technology represents the "doing" of the "Science of Being." This chapter will identify the language, logic, methods, techniques, and processes associated with specific applications of African American culture as restorative technology. It is written to provide examples of "restorative technologies" and paradigm shifting, nomenclature, terminology, and nosology as well as a radically new conception of restoration language, logic, and restorative portals for achieving wellness. The reconceptualization of culture[1] places the varied features (factors, aspects, and manifestations) of culture in functional order and suggests that culture be thought of as having a deep structure or cultural substance and a surface layer of cultural manifestations with the overall model being comprised conceptually as having three levels (see schema below). The deep structure of culture or cultural substance is composed of the factors and aspects of culture. The factors of culture are those elements or features which address a people's resolute "understanding" about the structure and origin of the universe (i.e., cosmology), the nature of being (i.e., ontology), and the natural character of universal relationships (i.e., axiology). Thus, cultural factors obviously influence a people's general design for living and patterns for interpreting reality. What emerges from these factors of culture is a people's "codification" of their implicitly cultural design. The deep structural codes which we have defined as the secondary and intermediary levels of culture are called cultural aspects. They are represented by a people's most comprehensive ideas about order, which some have defined as a people's worldview, their set or sets of guiding principles or ethos and their template for clarifying and giving perspective to their perceived social reality or ideology.

Unfortunately, what is most often understood as culture is, in actuality, the surface layer of culture or the manifestations or expressions of culture. These are the things like behavior, ideas, values, rituals, customs, language, for example, which mark a people's experience. The manifestations of culture should be viewed as the overt expressions of the aspects and factors of a people's cultural idiom. Hence, a complete understanding of a people's reality must occur by first understanding its factors (i.e., cosmology, ontology, and axiology); secondly, its emergent aspects (i.e., ethos, ideology, and worldview), and thirdly, its manifestations (i.e., customs, beliefs, behavior, language). It is both implicitly and explicitly suggested that the culture of a people and the values, attitudes, and behaviors consistent with it help to define, select, create, and re-create what is considered good, valuable, appropriate, or desirable and, conversely, what is bad, dangerous, inappropriate, or undesirable in their social milieu. Just as nothing human can be found outside of culture, so too, the meaning of everything human can be found only within one's culture. In the larger context, the "meaning" of a people's reality and the experiences within it are, in part, determined by the specific interplay between the cultural deep structure, surface-level manifestations, and the concrete historical conditions in which the people find themselves.

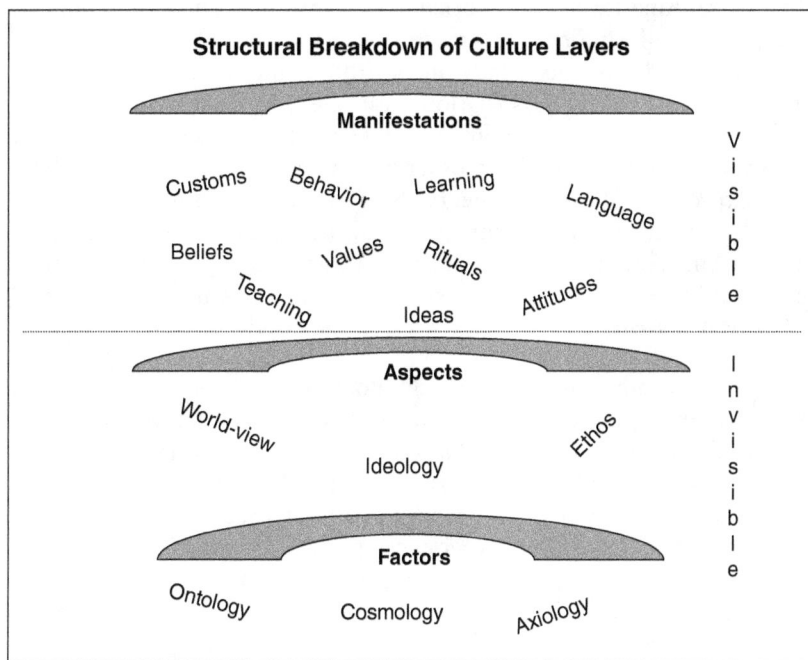

Structural Breakdown of Culture Layers

Manifestations

Customs   Behavior   Learning   Language

Beliefs   Values   Rituals

Teaching   Ideas   Attitudes

Visible

Aspects

World-view   Ethos

Ideology

Invisible

Factors

Ontology   Cosmology   Axiology

STRUCTURAL BREAKDOWN OF CULTURE

All cultural adoptions, adaptations, and exchanges occur at the manifestation level. However, it is the cultural factor and aspect levels, both of which are invisible, that give meaning and significance to what is visible (culturally manifested). In this sense, the cultural factors and aspects are most resistant to change. However, change is inevitable and happens at a very slow rate over several centuries. It is the cultural manifestations that are most susceptible to change, as they are based on reward and punishment contingencies. Contemporary African American culture should, in fact, be seen as a psycho-cultural, geopolitical complex composite of African cultural retentions and American social inventions expressed in a Eurocentric environment. Things that are punished will be changed; things that are rewarded will continue to exist.

African Americans, as a group, are, therefore, culturally complex. Despite the tremendous variety that exists among African American people, many African Americans continue to share elements of a common culture. African American life and living is grounded in both environmental conditions and a complex structure of cultural prerequisites, precepts, themes, norms, virtues, values, and customs.

The African American cultural orientation is grounded in a set of implicit precepts that inform or express themselves as recurring themes which, in turn, shape and influence behaviors, attitudes, and beliefs. Each precept has a primary or direct association with one or more recurring themes and an indirect or secondary impact on each of the others. Each precept is, however, connected to every other precept and contributes something to the expression of every theme. In effect, the cultural precepts influence the cultural themes that occur and re-occur in the life experiences of African American people. These characteristics are grounded both in African culture[2] and in the experiences that African Americans have had in North America.

The use of culture as restorative technology requires the specification of its specific precepts, themes, norms, customs, and metaphors (proverbial speech). The intrinsic precepts of a culture inform and express themselves as "rules or laws" which shape and influence behaviors, attitudes, and beliefs. The summary below is meant to be used as an initial reference to better understand the lived experiences of African American people by connecting particular precepts to the themes that influence behavior, attitudes, and beliefs. It has been suggested (Nobles, 1974) that eight precepts can be identified as influencing the indigenous culture in the traditional African American community. These eight precepts serve as the rules and laws for African American culture. The meaning of each precept is as follows: (1) *Consubstantiation*: This precept refers to the notion that pervades the African ethos that all elements of the universe are of one substance, that is, Spirit, and that all matter, whether animate or inanimate are merely different manifestations of the Godforce (Spirit). The peoples' approach to life is vitalistic rather than mechanistic. The precept of consubstantiation directly informs or influences the themes of spirituality and humanism. (2) *Interdependence*: This precept asserts that everything in the universe is connected. The precept of interdependence (everything is connected) directly informs or influences the themes of communalism and musicality and rhythm. (3) *Egalitarianism*: This precept asserts that the correct relationship between people is one of harmony and balance. The precept of egalitarianism, where human relationships are based on harmony and balance, directly informs or influences the themes of rhythm and realness. (4) *Collectivism*: This precept asserts that individual effort is a reflection or instrument of communal or collective survival and advancement. It is associated with two ideals—the greatest good for the greatest number of people, and a person is valued only to the degree that they contribute to the maintenance and survival of the community. "Whatever happens to the person, happens to the group; whatever happens to the group, happens to the person." The precept of collectivism (the group takes precedence over the individual) directly informs or influences the themes of communalism and realness. (5) *Transformation*: This precept asserts that everything has the potential to continually function at a higher level. It conceives of change as movement toward higher-level functioning. The precept of transformation (the process of becoming better) directly informs or influences the themes of resilience and orality and expressiveness. (6) *Cooperation*: This precept asserts that the optimal way of functioning is with mutual respect and encouragement. It recognizes that survival is predicated on the peoples' communalistic and collectivistic nature. Life is highly cooperative. There is no self outside the cultural community and even individual uniqueness is expressed within the milieu of the woven cultural fabric. The precept of cooperation (human relations are based on mutual respect and encouragement) directly informs or influences the theme of emotional vitality. (7) *Humanness*: This precept asserts that the whole world is vitalistic (alive) and that this vitality is grounded in a sense of goodness. To the African, the entire universe is vitalistic as opposed to mechanistic. This sense of vitality is infused into all areas of human activity. The precept of humanness (entire universe is vitalistic) directly informs or influences the themes of spirituality and humanism. (8) *Synergism*: This precept asserts that the performance outcomes of cooperative effort will be greater than the sum total of individual effort. People cooperate not just to gain fulfillment from working together, but to generate something greater than would be produced through individual effort, that is, synergy. The precept of synergy (the results of the total is greater than the sum total of individual effort leading to regenerations) directly informs or influences all of the individual themes.

White (1984) has identified nine cultural themes as being part and parcel to African American culture (e.g., the general design for living and patterns for interpreting reality) in the traditional African American community. These themes, which have been fully recognized as examples of authentic African American behavior, are as follows: (1) *Spirituality*—the belief that all elements of the universe are of one substance (Spirit) and that all matter, whether animate or inanimate, is merely different manifestations of the Godforce (spirit). (2) *Resilience*—the conscious need to bounce back from disappointment and disaster and to use the tools of humor and joy to renew and transform life's energy. This transformation, the process of becoming better, is informed by verve or the desire for creativity and antipathy for the mundane and monotonous. (3) *Egalitarianism*—a harmonious and balanced relationship between people in social systems and human affairs; the realization that the universe is made up of complementary yet opposite elements and that living is a creative synthesis of these elements. (4) *Communalism*—awareness of the interdependence of people and of the need to act in accordance with the notion that one's duty to one's family and social group is more important than one's individual privileges and rights. (5) *Orality and Verbal Expressiveness*—the attachment of special importance to knowledge that is passed on through word of mouth and the cultivation of oral virtuosity; a special sensitivity to aural modes of communication and a reliance on oral expression to convey meanings and feelings. (6) *Personal Style and Uniqueness*—the cultivation of a unique or distinct personality or essence; the desire to put one's own brand on an activity; approaching life as if it were one continuous artistic endeavor. (7) *Realness*—facing life as it is, without pretense; a contempt for artificiality and falseness in human conduct or for casualness in social transactions; an aversion to formality and standardization and preference for frankness of manner. (8) *Emotional Vitality*—a sense of aliveness, animation, and openness, conveyed via language, oral literature, song, dance, body language, folk poetry, and expressive thought. (9) *Musicality/Rhythm*—an appreciation and operationalization of the connectedness of movement, music, dance, percussiveness, and rhythm (the latter being the basic ingredient of African expressiveness); a rhythmic orientation toward life.

African American cultural norms are common standards or patterns of social behaviors that are typical of and expected by African American people. African American normative behavior, beliefs, and attitudes can be identified around nine critical life events: (1) birthing, (2) puberty (sexuality), (3) sisterhood/brotherhood, (4) wo/manhood, (5) marriage/bonding, (6) mothering/fathering, (7) eldership, (8) death (transition), (9) ancestor veneration.

Examples of African American Norms

- Protection Norm: Smudging the newborn infant and the wearing of an asafetida bag to ward off evil spirits and from people giving the child the "evil eye"

- Family Loyalty Norm: Told to not discuss your business with others; "Keep your business to yourself"; a rule in the family

- Transmission of Wisdom and Values Norm: Always called your elders Ms./Mr./ Sir/Ma'am or Auntie, Uncle

- Honoring Life Lived Norm: Pour a little liquor on the ground for those who have departed. "Talking the life lived" at funerals

- Right Conduct Norm: Never have romantic relationships with siblings' or friends' ex

African American customs are traditional and widely accepted ways of behaving or doing something that is specific to African American life and living in a particular place, or time. African American customs are expressed or found in the following seven critical life areas or moments: (1) health and healing, (2) education, (3) childrearing/socialization, (4) cooking, (5) worship/religion, (6) work/productivity, (7) creativity/ arts/aesthetic.

Examples of African American Customs

- Purification Custom: "Once a year all the children had to line up and get a dose of Castor Oil. The purpose was to 'clean' you out and keep you well. This was done the first week after school was out for the end of the year."

- Perfectibility Custom: "Traditionally, it used to be that at the beginning of the school year on the first day of school, Mommas would 'polish' you up (supposedly as a fight against ashiness). The underlying belief was that if you shined on the outside you would shine on the inside (the mind or intelligence). The fight against ashiness was a custom for priming the pump of excellence."

METAPHORICAL AND PROVERBIAL SPEECH

Use of metaphor and proverbial speech are African cultural retentions and a direct inventive outgrowth of African American response to oppression and dehumanization in racist White America. African American cultural and spiritual nuances are especially found or revealed in the use of metaphor, which is a figure of speech in which a word or phrase that designates one thing or idea really represents a deeper appreciation of the underlying values, beliefs, and ethos of a people's culture and sense of humanity.

As expressions of cultural and spiritual nuance, Metaphoric discourse serves to

- Advance and assert personhood
- Clarify circumstances
- Establish situational control and illumination

Through the use of cultural and spiritual metaphors, African Americans seek, project, and protect personhood in the quest to be the cause and the consequence of joy, beauty, and productivity (creativity).

Metaphorical and proverbial speech represent strategies for dealing with life situations. They involve implicit generalizations or observations

Proverbial and Metaphorical Schema

Cultural and Spiritual Nuances			
Mental Health Underpinnings of Metaphoric Discourse			
	Belief	Attitude	Behavior
Advancing/ Asserting Personhood	The blacker the berry, the sweeter the juice. Beauty is skin deep but ugliness is to the bone. Once you go Black, you never go back. I'll get the right one and the wrong one. What goes up, comes down.	Don't be no educated fool. You've got to work twice as hard to get half as much. I brought you into the world and I can take you out. You have to be twice as good to get half as much. Don't get high on you own supply.	God don't like ugly. Keep what you got and share what you have. Don't write no checks your behind can't cash. Keep on keepin' on. Up to it, down to it, dogs to it, and stick to it. If you can't do it, let me do it because I'm use to it. Birds of a feather fly together.
Clarifying Circumstance	All eyes closed ain't asleep. A little education is a dangerous thing. Common sense ain't so common. Use your mother wit. What is understood need not be said. A hard head makes a soft ass. The grass ain't always green on the other side of the fence.	You don't pay for you own raising till you raise your own. Fair exchange ain't no robbery. I'm not crazy as I am foolish dressed. Mediocrity is a White man's luxury. Put your brain in a gnat and the gnat will fly backward. What is White ain't always right. You a lie and the truth ain't in you. History is a mystery.	What goes around comes around. Money talks— bullshit walks. Children shouldn't play with sharp tools without adult supervision. There are two types of criminals: the one caught and the uncaught.

Cultural and Spiritual Nuances			
Mental Health Underpinnings of Metaphoric Discourse			
	Belief	Attitude	Behavior
Situational Control/ Illumination	The pot calling the kettle black. Don't let the little head rule the big head. Perfect can't be the enemy of the good. You think fat meat ain't greasy.	Can't see the forest for looking at the trees. A closed mouth doesn't get fed.	May the valleys be made high and the mountains made low. One monkey don't stop no show. Children should be seen and not heard. I will fight until the well freezes over and then I will turn around and fight you for the ice. You know where you been . . . but you don't know where you are going. Don't pee in my face and tell me it's raining.

presented in connection with particular events. The form which the proverbs take, the context within which they are used, and the content integrated within them combine to provide meaning to a particular value orientation and behavioral disposition. Proverbs have always been used by African/Black people. For the most part, African/Black people used proverbs to specifically reinforce the installation of certain values, attitudes, and ethics in our children. As an expressive tool for character development, proverbs can be used to reveal the underlying principles which govern role behavior. The proverb makes explicit the purpose of one's existence, the natural order of things, and the way we should relate to each other. For example, we can ask, "What does the proverb 'The man on his feet carries off the share of the man sitting down' mean for how Black men should relate to working and training or personal responsibilities?" Proverbs make explicit the purpose of one's existence, the natural order of things, and the way we should relate to each other. As such they represent a people's general disposition toward the world. Proverbs also represent strategies for dealing with life situations. The proverb "The strong person builds a path for the weak one to walk on," relates to the cultural theme of cooperation.

Proverbial speech includes implicit generalizations or observations presented in connection with particular events. The form includes a specific observation, implying a general truth, which bears on a particular event. An alternative form is a general observation referring to a specific event. For example, "What goes around comes around," is a general observation of connections between events which may be used to remind an individual to expect appropriate consequences for his behavior. More commonly, the proverb takes the specific to general form: "The price of your hat ain't the measure of your brain" is a specific observation, implying a general truth (i.e., external symbols are unreliable indicators of personal resources). The form which the proverb takes, the context within which it is used, and the content integrated within it combine to provide meaning to a particular value orientation and behavioral disposition. Proverbs are like analogies. The analogic process focuses on the identification of relationships or similarities among experiences. Thus animal life is analogous to plant life; thinking is analogous to living. Analogies can be identified among all experiences. Analogies identify and reinforce connections toward the objective of integrating all phenomena in an interdependent scheme (synthesis).

The question of African American culture cannot be complete without recognizing that African American culture includes both historical "retentions" and contemporary "inventions." Sometimes cultural retentions are thought of as the old ways and the cultural inventions as the new cultural forms or practices that each new generation creates and adds to the cultural treasury and repertoire. The cultural retentions should be thought of as those practices, procedures, products, or protocols that have been retained across time and place, that is, Black music (gospel, jazz, R & B, hip-hop); method or style of worship; protocols of eldership; dietary habits, cooking attitude and style; and language structure and use (Ebonics). All of these various retentions serve as the bases of the various and ongoing development of African American cultural inventions; hands up in church, high sign in sports, the "Almighty Look," intergenerational childrearing practices, African American aesthetic (style), arm double-crossing (in death, Rapper's stance), left foot forward, use of "Yo," meaning thought or will which takes form (comes) from itself, improvisation (in most performance, music, and sports), African American aesthetic, Black woman's neck motion and hands on her hips, service and sacrifice, Kwanzaa, self-cherishment and collective cherishment, new salutations and greetings of familial entitlement, like uncle, auntie. In the tension between the old and the new as well as insider and outsider perspectives, many cultural expressions are often perceived as regionally limited or stereotypical. Traditional African American cultural values alone consist of respect for elders, race pride, collective responsibility, restraint, devotion, reciprocity, patience, cognitive flexibility, courage, resilience, defiance, integrity, self-mastery, persistence, and productivity.

Culture, nevertheless, tells us what experiences mean and that there are "correct" interpretations that emerge from and were developed by the group and must be used when explaining a given experience or experiences. Within this body of interpretations are ideas about "how life is" and "how the world works," and ideas about the causes that underlie phenomena, events, and behavior. Proverbial and metaphorical speech are epistemic reflections and conclusions.

ENDNOTES

1. Nobles's conceptualization of culture asserts that culture can be constructed as having three levels: (1) cultural factors which serve as the grounding for ideas and concepts that are organized into core beliefs about nature of being and reality, including the universe, deity and nature, the structure of being and the nature of relationships, among elements in the universe; (2) cultural aspects which serve to shape a people's ethos (tone, character and quality of life, as well as their moral and aesthetic style and mode); worldview (an understanding of events in the world and the purpose of the world as a whole); and ideology (informs the creation of the ideas and concepts about human life and living); and (3) cultural manifestations which are what we are able to see and openly experience such as values, attitudes, behavior, customs, language, traditions, beliefs, rituals, inventions. The most obvious manifestation of a people's culture is their behavior.

2. The major cultural and linguistic lineages for African American people are the BaNtu-Kongo (see Fu-Kiau, 1980; Holloway, 1991; Kuyk, 2003).

VII

The Application of African American Cultural Restorative Technology

African American culture with its precepts, customs, values, traditions, and rituals are the technology for doing the being of African people. *Culture*[1] is the term for the process or template that reflects the vast structure of behaviors, ideas, attitudes, values, habits, beliefs, customs, language, rituals, and practices that give people a *general design for living and patterns for interpreting reality*. For all human beings, culture, through its shared historical experience and its compelling description of a preferred future (vision), not only influences but actually determines human interests. It is this cultural vision that incites emotion and compels commitment and informs a cultural group about what is good and what is not good for it. The cultural vision of humans, in fact, describes how conditions can be improved, which almost always includes the superimposition of what was thought to be good from the past. Culture tends to preserve itself.

While all humans live in culture, every cultural community, due to their unique set of environmental challenges and historical experiences, has a special cultural vision or imprint (manifestation). It is this cultural imprint or vision that validates cultural behavior and cultural products. Particular cultural imprints bind individuals together as a group and empower that group to name or label themselves, whether that name or label is a simple "we" or "the people" or "beings" or "most folks" or whatever name the group decides gives the best representation of their group identity. People who have been bound together by culture, who have developed a sense of group identity, and who have conformed to the fundamental beliefs and standards derived from the long-standing customs and traditions of that culture, comprise an identifiable cultural community.

African American culture as a dynamic system of features, factors, and functions with sets of guiding principles, assumptions, conventions, beliefs, and rules that permit and determine how African Americans relate to each other and develop their creative potential can be reframed as restorative technology.

LANGUAGING AND UTILIZATION OF *SKH DJR*

I, parenthetically, want to explain my use of traditional African languages to represent the scientific "concepts" that emerge from the recommended African paradigm and episteme. Not only is this consistent with the dictates of the proposed new discourse, it is appropriate as an act of authenticity or authority. The use of African language terminology is critical to the reclaiming of African-centered discourse. In this regard, I (Nobles et al., 2016) point out that "concepts can be misconstrued or not fully understood or developed when they are defined, interpreted or constructed using a language not specific to the particular culture." Concepts reflect or represent phenomena within a particular culture. Every language reflects and represents some particular people's culture. Given African peoples' sensitivity to the "power" of the word, *Nommo*, we more than most people recognize that words have transformative power in that they are capable of legitimizing the material manifestation of phenomena. Concepts, represented by words, can and do have the ability to reinforce or reject the cultural moorings or foundations of a cultural community. African American theorists should be especially sensitive to the words used in constructing their theory. When one uses a language that is hostile or irrelevant to the cultural system under examination, then the concepts, via the language, will severely limit the understanding of the phenomena within that culture (1995, p. 7). I believe that when the African theorists utilize non-African concepts (i.e., Latin, Greek, Roman, Anglo-Saxon) to represent the social phenomena of African life, they unknowingly incorporate the psychological energy (via subliminal meanings) associated with these concepts and thereby create "false positives" in the discoveries of African American conduct. The African researcher should, at every possibility, use African concepts to describe and give meaning to African phenomena.

Accordingly, for the Sonay people of Mali, the word for black is "bibi" (Maiga, 1996, p. 17). *Bibi* is actually a concept used to refer to the essential goodness of things. It is never used to refer to anything negative or inferior. The full significance of this concept is found in the expression, *wayne bibi* (black sun). Dr. Maiga (1996, p. 18) notes that the Gao people of Mali use the term *wayne bibi* to refer to the hottest part of the day when the sun is at its fullest. In effect, *wayne bibi* refers to the fullest expression of the sun. It is when the sun is the brightest, the most dazzling and the most radiant. The black sun symbolizes luminosity, the state of being unlimited, and the condition that when a thing achieves its total expression. Similarly, the Sonay people use the term *Ay moo hari bibi* (Give me black water) to signify water that is from the sun.

Before further discussing the philosophical grounding Skh, the Science of Being, I want to highlight the importance of language as defined by Diop's (1974) directive to find the cultural unity of Africa by examining the domains of history, language, and psyche and the significance of the BaNtu heritage. Diop (1974, p. xiii) makes a convincing argument that the cultural unity of Africa is located in its language, history, and psyche. Africa has over 3,000 indigenous languages and innumerable creoles, pidgins, and lingua francas. The idea that Africa is a land of Babel was used to support the idea that those Africans kidnapped into slavery all spoke many different languages and were not able to understand each other. However, what is more accurate is that most languages spoken in Africa belong to one of three large language families, that is, Afroasiatic, Nilo-Saharan, and Niger-Congo (Epstein & Kole, 1998). The Niger-Congo language family, in my opinion, should be termed the BaNtu-Kongo language family. It is the migratory expansion of the BaNtu[2] with their language, beliefs, and so on, and not the river Niger that more accurately denotes the language family. Parenthetically, the so-called Niger-Congo, or, more correctly, BaNtu-Kongo, represents about three-fourths of all of sub-Saharan Africa. With regard to language families, what should be obvious but seemingly less appreciated is that people create language to communicate about what is most important to them, that is, environment, experience, belief, thought, and so on. The BaNtu-Kongo language family represents the need of the BaNtu people to communicate their thoughts, beliefs, and experiences. Hence, if there is a common language family, then there must be common experiences, environment, beliefs, and thoughts that bind that language family. It should also be noted here that BaNtu essentially means people or the people of spirit (*Ntu*). However, it has been denigrated, especially in South Africa and, refers now to be a qualifier designating inferior status or the area, that is, BaNtustan, set aside for Black people in support of apartheid.

Consistent with Diop's (1974) directive to examine the domains of history, language, and psyche, *Skh* would require that one interrogate the language and logic of traditional African people in order to gain insight into the functioning of contemporary African peoples. Our ancestors were spread throughout the diaspora absent of freedom, that is, in chains. However, they did not arrive absent of language, thought, and belief about who they were. Our ancestors on the continent had a sacred relation to the land. However, because of colonial domination, that relationship was often disrupted. One direct consequence of colonialism was that many African children were forced into boarding schools and had to learn their captor's language as well as their "way of being." They too did not experience this atrocity absent of their mother tongue, thought, and belief about who they were. Our ancestors came with a language and a system of beliefs (logic) about what it meant to be human and to whom, whose they are, and why they existed. It is through a penetrating reinterpretation of the language and logic of our African ancestry that both continental and diasporan Africans will be able to rescue and remember our humanity, wholeness, and wellness.

In directing us to locate Africa's cultural unity in its language, history, and psyche, Diop unfortunately left the exploration of the psychic unity undone. In an attempt to partially address Diop's psychic directive, I have offered the concept or notion of *Skh Sdi* (Sah koo Shedee) to represent the practice or method of *Sakhu* (Sah koo) first introduced by Akbar (1985). Consistent with the African idea of "If it exists, it most assuredly is spirit," the *Skh Sdi* practitioners would be "Spirits (humans) who are 'lead' by spirit, who 'read' spirit(s); and seeks help and protection from spirit and engages in the 'salvation' and 'nurturing' (healing) of spirit by performing the Sakhu as it should be done" (Nobles, 2013, p. 294). There are traditional African concepts in every African language that represent the idea of illuminating the spirit and should be explored as a further expansion of a Pan African Black psychology.

The evolving Pan African Black psychology, as *Skh*, the Science of Being, should be an African-centered interdisciplinary and multidimensional investigation of African philosophy, literature, languages, history, politics, aesthetics, spirituality, and science. As a global discipline, *Skh*, the Science of Being would allow us to approach questions of human essence, experience, and expressions (i.e., values, customs, beliefs, conduct) important to all cultures—the nature of the beautiful, the meaning of human existence, the search for the divine, the nature of historical epochs—through the interdisciplinary and multidimensional illuminating, *Skh* studies.

AFRICAN LANGUAGE AND LOGIC

African people (both continental and diasporan), though often disrespected or unrecognized, have always possessed full languages and systems of beliefs (logic) about what it means to be human. The importance of language is fundamental. In fact, in discussing the African origins of civilization, traditional language is particularly important because in the language of traditional philosophy is found ancient words and phrases that illuminate the psyche.

One of the most contestable issues in Western psychology is the view that African languages are not sufficiently developed to be used in science. Science is, however, not value free, nor is it apolitical (Hindess, 1996; Mkhize, 2004; Nagel, 1961). To reason things African or Asian, using a foreign language is problematic. This is because any language is the bearer of a specific epistemological paradigm. The reasoning that underlies a particular language espouses an epistemological paradigm that is not necessarily the same for all existing paradigms. In this sense, rendering African experiences in a foreign language such as English is potentially opening the door for a clash of epistemological paradigms. This clash is not the basis for affirming the one language as scientific and the other as nonscientific. It is through the penetrating reinterpretation of the language and logic of our African ancestry that Africans (both continental and diasporan) will be able to rescue and remember our humanity, wholeness, and wellness.

The language and logic of Africa, particularly the BaNtu-Kongo languages, are replete with examples of concepts that represent both language and logic. For instance, the word *khotso* means a wish for peace for the community, starting with the greeted person acknowledging the wish for peace of body, spirit, and mind. The word *Bushukudi/kushukula* represents an intellectual activity that is realized in the language from the verb *ku-shuku-la*, from which two words are derived: first, the abstract word *bushu-kudi* or *bu-di-juku*, which means "clarification," "laid bare," "elucidation," "enlightenment," and so on. The second word, *shushukulu* (var. *muju-kudi*), denotes "one who knows the foundations of something," "one that can release the taproot of a fact or a problem." The word *Nkindi* refers to both *subject* and *object*. When applied to the subject, it means *shushukulu*, or specialist in the creation and development of deep "thought" or an "idea," *Nkindi* is a specialist or a scholar in the art or way of thinking.

Epistemic justice recognizes that within every language there is embedded the logic of the people's understanding of human roles, relationships, and responsibilities. Epistemic justice demands that appropriate language must be used if one is to conduct a profound and penetrating search, study, and mastery of the process of "illuminating" the human spirit or essence, ergo, *Skh Djr.* Friend-du-Preez et al. (2009) agrees that illuminating the human spirit can be found in the language of the BaNtu-Kongo. The African term *ukufakwabantu* (isiZulu) is thought to literally mean "diseases of the people" (Friend-du Preez et al., 2009). However, *uku* means "to" and *kwabantu* refers to the ancestors. Hence, the underlying logic of the language here would lead us to understand the word, *uku-fakwabantu*, to refer to more than diseases of a people, but to spirit-related illnesses or spirit damage found among the ancestors (in the invisible realm, the macrocosmos), as well as among the people in the visible realm, the microcosmos.

African salutations or greetings have an implicit logic within African language. A deeper understanding of African salutations or greetings is further demonstrative of African reality and its importance in the context of therapy. Concepts such as *ditumediso* (greetings), *ubuntu/botho/vunhu* (humanness), *badimo* (living dead), and *semoya* (spirituality) are informative. In seSotho and seTswana, *ditumediso* (greetings) have an ontologically meaningful role in the lives of African people. One way in which Africans demonstrate their *ubuntu/botho/vunhu* (humanity) is through *ditumediso* (greetings). All things are inseparably connected (Akbar, 2016, p. 18; Nobles, 1986a, p. 58). In the Twi language of the Fante/Asante people, the greeting *Wohotesen* (wo-ho-te-sen) means more than "Hello" or "How are you?" Its deeper meaning is "I lower myself before you" or "I bow down before your essence." It demonstrates that in meeting, I recognize, respect, and honor the value of your essence or spirit. *Ditumediso* function as a practical recognition of this inseparable connectedness. They do so by acknowledging the triadic structure of community understood from an African perspective, namely, the living, the living dead, and the yet-to-be-born (Ramose, 2002, p. 77). When Africans greet each other, the health of *setshaba* or community is the basic concern. For Africans, greetings cannot be divorced from the living dead, *badimo/abaphansi*, who are believed to be responsible ontologically. *Dumelang*, which translates to "agree," or *sanibonani* in isiZulu, which literally means that *we see you*. The *-ng* and *sani-* denote the plural of agree, and *we see you* is already in the plural. The *we* refers to the triadic conception of community. The addressee of the greeting responds, for example, by either *ahe* or *le lena dumelang*. The former means that the greeting is acknowledged. The latter is the reciprocation of the greeting requesting the initial interlocutor to also agree, again in the plural sense. This is then followed by *le kae?* Literally translated as *Where are you?*, *le kae* recognizes the immediate locative position of *motho,* the human being. *Where are you?* is redundant because the person greeted is seen literally to be in the specific physical location in which they are. This leads to the subtle and critical meaning of *le kae?* The ethical meaning of *le kae?* is precisely "Where do you stand?" or "How is your relationship with the community at present?" The point of this question is that harmonious relations with the community amount to good health, whereas ill health is the experience of disharmony (pathology) in one's relations with the community. The addressee affirms good health when they respond *re gona/teng,* literally translated as *We are here.* However, the ethical meaning of *re gona* is that harmony prevails in the communal relations, meaning we are mutually enjoying good health.

RECOMMENDED LANGUAGING SHIFTING

Nganga (instead of *therapist*); **Ngang'a nkisi** (en-gang-gah en-kee-see), (healer) is capable of activating the process by which the body (persons or community) repairs, cures, or restores itself to health and well-being—one who restores the physical, psychic, social and cosmic balance and harmony in and between persons, people (community), nature and the Divine, and one who cures both physical and spiritual disease and serves as a powerful mediator between the visible world and the realm of spirit and ancestors. **Bwana Mboti** (instead of *client*); **Bwana Mboti** (bwah-nah em-boh-tee), the child of my Ancestors; **Mbevu** (instead of *patient*); **Mbevu** (em-beh-voo), a sick or unhealthy person; **N'tènda** (instead of *clinical director*); **N'tènda** (en-tehn-dah), a guide for healers, this person oversees the process; **Mbut'a N'niakisa** (instead of *clinical supervisor*); **Mbut'a N'niakisa** (em-boo-tah en-nee-ah-kee-sah), one who guides the N'niakisi; **Sumuna** (instead of Trauma), and **Sumununu** (en-soo-moo-noo-noo), when the spirit of the community and the spirit of its members become defiled or damaged; (KiKongo) **Jegna** (instead of *mentor*); *Jegna* (jehg-nah), special people (*Jegnoch*, plural form) who have (1) been tested in struggle or battle, demonstrated extraordinary and unusual fearlessness, (2) shown determination and courage in protecting our people, land, and culture, (3) shown diligence and dedication to our people, (4) produced exceptionally high-quality work, and (5) dedicated themselves to the protection, defense, nurturance, and development of our young by advancing our people, place, and culture—the easiest and foremost interpretation of the *Jegna* is one whose central focus is on the culture and character of one's people, and the *Jegnoch* cherish and love their (our) people (Ethiopian/Amharic); **Makolo** (instead of *confused*); **Makolo** (Mah-koh-loh), spiritual knots; **Kizungu Zungo,** *Kizungu Zungu* (kee-zoon-goo zoon-goo), the defiled or damaged spirits (individual or collective) seen as "tornadoes of the mind" or "mental chaos" (not insanity/mental illness); *Ngolo,* energy of self-healing power; *Ngolo* (en-goh-loh), energy of self-healing power in our "genetic code" and that wellness is in our DNA (KiKongo); *Zola ZOLA* (love) *Zola* (zoh-lah), magnetic energy with an electrical charge that makes contact and connection between knowing and knowable spirits (energy) to cause the activation of NGOLO (healing energy)—the energy that causes the activation of molecular or cellular regeneration at both the material and immaterial levels; and **Personhood** instead of *individual*.

Hence, with appropriate respect for African "languaging" as our scientific terminology, we can now turn to the task of translating these ideas into "doings" that are offered as examples of cultural restorative technologies.

ENDNOTES

1. It is further asserted that culture is as essential to human life as water is to living fish. Culture is not simply the song and dance of a people. Nor is it merely the compilation of their holidays and rituals or the listing of their heroes and heroines. For all human beings, culture gives meaning to reality. It is the total environmental reality. As such, culture has the power to compel behavior and the capacity to reinforce ideas and beliefs about all aspects of human functioning, including mental health, educational achievement, motivation, and development. Culture is the invisible medium that encompasses all human existence. It is important to note that nothing human happens outside of culture. What binds all cultural transactions are, however, agreements. Culture itself is a product of the agreements among human beings who share historical experiences; who have come together as a group; who hold common beliefs and affix certain values and meanings to people, events, and behaviors. Culture also tells its members what and how to behave and gives them a vision of what they may become as a result of following and abiding by its dictates. It does this by presenting to its members compelling descriptions of a preferred future for the cultural group. It is this vision that the members of the cultural group rally around.

2. The primary evidence for this great expansion (Ehret, 2001), one of the largest in human history, has been linguistic, namely that the languages spoken in sub-Equatorial Africa are remarkably similar to each other, to the degree that it is unlikely that they began diverging from each other more than 3,000 years ago. The BaNtu people with their culture, language, family, spiritual beliefs, and philosophical ideas are the very people stolen and kidnapped in the Transatlantic slave trade. In effect, BaNtu beliefs and ideas were embedded in the various peoples who were stolen and kidnapped.

VIII

Restorative Praxis Technologies

The aim or goal of restoration is to enable a (be)ing (person) to understand cosmic life and the primacy of affirming life, and to understand one's place and role as family and community. As a cosmic being (manifestation), one is to gain various skills and abilities necessary to become a contributing member of the family/community.

ZAYA DISCOURSE

Zaya (v) is a KiKongo term meaning to know, imagine. This ancient term was rescued, expanded, and reinterpreted as *Zaya Discourse*, meaning the ability to remember and imagine additional authentic culturally congruent (African-centered) thoughts, ideas, and knowing stimulated by communal conversation. Zaya helps reveal what was lost or distorted as well as assists in creating "signposts" (imagination and memory) for reclaiming our way and restoring wellness going forward. Zaya Discourse depends on "memory" (identifying, recalling, and rescuing ideas, beliefs, values, customs, and experiences) and "imagination" (co-creating wonderment around new and refined ideas, beliefs, behaviors, values, customs, activities, and experiences).

As part of the African-centered paradigm shift, the restoration process will engage in Zaya Discourse.[1] Zaya Discourse is an intentional culturally congruent (African-centered) process designed for African and African ancestry restoration of wellness. The *Zaya Discourse process* is an openly and unapologetically, culturally congruent (African-centered) initiative designed in alignment with African and African ancestry cultural reality and *Skh Tm* (advanced Pan African Black psychology). The Zaya Discourse process will enable African and African ancestry therapeutic programs and clinical in-service trainings to work in more culturally congruent (African-centered) ways with African and African ancestry populations. Zaya Talk Discourse requires a deep and profound understanding of African and African ancestry culture and worldview and ways of Being. Our clinical in-services are designed to intentionally co-activate, instigate, and reinforce the reharmonization of the disconnects by being able to see oneself in the other (recognition of other as oneself). It opens and guides the creation of harmonization (knitting back together, realigning, etc.) and mending desperate, antagonistic, and damaging elements or energies and experiences.

Stimulated by mutual engagement that is grounded in the decolonization of thinking (minds) and the affirmation of being African, Zaya Discourse emphasizes African-centered languaging, narrative, and voice in alignment with African and African ancestral cultural beliefs and values and *Skh Tm* (advanced Pan African Black psychology).

Through this African-centered conversational technique, participants are not only able to engage in open, courageous, and honest conversations, but they are also able to take advantage of cross-over talk and, conversationally, inspire unscripted responses that generate and clarify thoughts and opinions. This process allows for following through or following up on ideas and thoughts relative to the discussions and exploring memory and imagination as "imaginings" in more depth. By way of Zaya Talk the co-discussants adopt an "inspirational" participatory stance to co-invent a new narrative. Specifically, the Zaya Talk will intentionally and collectively develop and design authentic (African-centered) culturally grounded (African-centered) agency-specific policy, planning, services, techniques, and programming.

The Zaya Discourse technique is designed to serve as a method for the restoration of the ability to activate the "mending of spirit damage/ disconnect." It allows for the participants to experience life and living as informed by the visible and invisible realms of reality and being well as characterized by confidence, competence, and a sense of full possibility and unlimited potentiality. As part of the African-centered paradigm shift, the restoration process should engage in Zaya Discourses. Every behavioral modality (talking, dancing, singing, walking, drumming, humming) and expression of feeling (meditation, imagining, communing with nature, deep breathing, interactions, especially playing with children, listening to [interviewing] elders) can be the source of Zaya Discourse.

ZOLA UP ON US: FIVE-STAR FAMILY ENHANCEMENT PLAN

This Restoration technique is designed as a hands-on interactive tool workbook to help create ways and activities that intentionally guide families' focus on being well. Through the workbook, families engage in activities in the five-star plan to remember, remind, reframe, revitalize, and reward what activates the life capacity to heal and be well. This process, in workbook format, as a restorative technique is formatted as multiple strategies (Five-Star Zola Up on Enhancing Our Family; Eight-Point Resurrecting Our Community; ten Principles of Personhood Right Conduct; two Fundamental Rules of Culture; and Living the Virtuous Life). Participants are encouraged to work collectively through the entire process and then select one of the clustered strategies to work through with family. Be creative. Be fearless and unapologetic and unashamed in your Zola "uppin" on Us. What do any of the strategies look like through your family's and your eyes? How do you do Zola as a dance, spoken word, game, or other performance? The first and main strategy is the Zola up on Us Five-Star Family Enhancement Plan. Our African ancestors knew and understood that Zola (love) is an energy or power that can and does "activate" our self-healing power (potential), which is called *Ngolo*. Then, as follow-up and follow-through, share what you have created with the rest of the family and community.

THERAPIST-IN-RESIDENCY

The *Skh-NgaNga-MBonGi* (also known as Therapist-in-Residency [TnR]) is a radically new and visionary African-centered mental health training program that changes the healing paradigm from the falsely claimed universal Western healing framework to an African-centered culturally congruent framework designed particularly for people of African ancestry. The formal title of the Therapist-in-Residency idea has been trademarked as "Skh-NgaNga-MBonGi™: An African-Centered Therapist-in-Residency."[2] This training program is grounded in principles of Black psychology (Nobles, 1986a, 2006) and African-centered approaches. More specifically, professionals of African ancestry supervise trainees of African ancestry who will provide mental health services at TnRP community-based organization (CBO) partner sites in Black communities. The overall goal of the TnRP initiative is to recruit and train licensed-eligible, mental health practitioners (master and doctoral levels) in the science of Black psychological therapeutic practice in order to deploy teams of mental health (Black psychology) practitioners to selected community-based organizations that are addressing and being affected by community crises. The TnR process directly and specifically assists in the restoration of wellness for African American persons, families, and communities.

The idea of a community-based Therapist-in-Residency process was created by the senior leadership of the Institute for the Advanced Study of Black Family Life and Culture, Inc., Drs. Wade Nobles and Lawford Goddard, almost a decade ago. In collaboration with Dr. Theopia Jackson, the idea was further operationalized within the context of mental health training. The implementation of the TnR idea was conducted by the Bay Area Chapter of the Association of Black Psychologists (BACABPsi) through the clinical expertise of Drs. Tony Jackson and Sandra Smith. With support from the California Endowment, the BACABPsi has been able to rigorously assess and validate the idea of a community-based Therapist-in-Residency process as a new and innovative culturally congruent (African-centered) healing practice. The Therapist-in-Residency idea is a radically new, innovative, and visionary community-based African-centered mental health program dedicated to providing culturally grounded mental health services for persons of African ancestry. Through the utilization of the science of Black psychology, African American culture, and the specific adoption of African language terms and healing logic, the *Skh-NgaNga-MBonGi*: An African-Centered Therapist-in-Residency Training idea reflects a bold "paradigm shifting" and institutionalization of an African-centered narrative for the restoration of wellness for African American persons, families, and community.

TnRP guiding principles are articulated as theoretical knowledge and application grounded in tenets of Black psychology or African-centered approaches, and how these inform the development of the *Nganga* (therapist). The TnRP critically interrogates or modifies African-centered theoretical models for their effectiveness with persons of African ancestry. It is a direct demonstration of the transmission, modification, or creation of approaches, methods, and conceptualizations that are directly informed by tenets of Black psychology or an African-centered worldview, values, practices, and beliefs. The grounding of TnRP in the Science of Being, ergo, *Skh Djr* and African American cultural precepts and orientations, along with the specific adoption of African language terms and healing logic, supports our adoption of a new and different transformative restorative praxis that we call *Alasal Tarey,* which in the Songhoy-senni language means "the process through which one comes to know and understand one's origin, essence and unfolding as a human being in order to serve humanity." Restoration as healing is intimately connected to the full knowing, understanding, and unfolding of one's being as a spirit being. Through engaging in *Alasal Tarey*, TnRP will further interrogate the role and function of healer (*Ntoki, Nganga*) and alternative diagnostic and treatment plans[3] as well as explore African and African-centered languages and logic of healing, terminology, nosology, classifications; healing rituals, ceremonies, strategies, and spoken medicine (proverbial). Ultimately, the African-centered paradigm shifting where participants include persons (inter-, intra-, and supra-) family, community, and a whole people (not individual clients and therapists) is to *Alasal Tarey*. The points and places wherein restorative pathways emerge, relate, and intersect via harmonization and regeneration (fractalization, synapsis/synergy-micro/macro) via the use of African-centered healing language, logic, nosology, and taxonomy with the assistance of sound (drumming) and motion (dance).

RECHARGING *SAKHU* ENERGY

The Recharging *Sakhu* Energy restorative technique[4] is a reharmonizing intervention designed to realign the relational space for personhood (self) or neighborhood (family and community) and activate *Sakhu* energy as the self-healing power to be well with confidence, competence, and a sense of full possibility and unlimited potentiality. This restoration technique utilizes the Akan Adinkra symbols cards. The idea of *Sakhu* energy posits that there is a knowing and knowable spirit which when tapped into informs our understanding and ability to heal. Based on the concept of *Skh Djr* that examines and utilizes the processes that allow for the illumination and liberation of the spirit and requires one to think deeply and profoundly about African meanings and understandings about being human. Activating *Sakhu* energy requires profound, deep thought, and reflection. Understood as "emblematic symbolism," the Adinkra symbolic drawings should be viewed as representing the idea that symbols invoke a complexity of ideas and feelings as well as an array of metaphoric meanings that are communicated as hidden episteme, that is, embedded knowing and knowledge. Adinkra symbols are symbolic drawings of concepts, values, proverbs, and philosophy developed by ancient Akan and Gyaaman peoples in the 16th century. The deeper meaning of **Kra** in Adin**KRA** can be found in the language and logic of Asante Twi. The African Spirit as reflected in the language and logic of Asante Twi suggests that the Akan consider a human being to be fundamentally spirit or force or energy comprised of three elements. The first element is the *OKRA*, which constitutes the innermost self, the essence of the person (Gyekye, 1997, p. 9). The **OKRA** is considered the living soul of the person and is sometimes referred to as the **OKRA**teasafo. As the living soul, the **OKRA** is identical with life. It is also the embodiment and transmitter of the individual's **NKRA**bea (destiny). The **NKRA**bea is a directing energy that can influence consciousness and orient one to one's purpose and meaning in life.

Accordingly, **KRA** in Adin**KRA** could be interpreted as the determinative for the set of symbols that provide a hidden language for revealing the simultaneous essence and purpose of life and living as the good and beautiful. As symbolic imagery, the Adin**KRA** symbols represent and reflect an Africana episteme wherein singularly and as a whole, the Adin**KRA**s refers to the nature of knowing, understanding, and being acquainted with aspects of reality that give justification, explanation, and rationality for belief. Metaphorically, **KRA** could also stand or point to results in Key Result Areas of life. In reading the Adin**KRA** symbols, one could therefore look for meaning associated with resultant condition(s) in some key areas of life and living; that is, behavior, beliefs, values, and attitudes.

ENDNOTES

1. The *Zaya Discourse* process is informed by the "semi-structured culturally grounded conversational (SSGGC) information gathering technique" created by Nobles and Goddard (circa 2017). More accurately the SSGGC has been elevated to a *Zaya Discourse*.

2. The Therapist-in-Residency is trademarked and is the intellectual property of Drs. Wade Nobles and Lawford Goddard. It is not to be duplicated and/or replicated in any form or fashion without written authorization.

3. One such diagnostic and treatment plan in development is called ASIM, which stands for *African Symbiotic Illumination Manual*. This manual is being designed to incorporate African classificatory terminology as guides for a restorative praxis.

4. The Re-charging *Sakhu* Energy restorative technique is based in the Adinkra cards developed by Dr. Erica Mapule McInnis.

IX

Summation/Beginning

While this book has been written as a kind of "scaffolded mindscaping travel log," it should be interpreted as an illumination textbook or guide for the rescue, reclamation, and refinement of the derailed African intellectual trajectory that leads to and speaks to the Science of Being. The intellectual dilemma found in accepting the need to know and understand both the visible and invisible realms and to know what the knowing and knowable spirit knows is undaunting. The Western paradigm and framework imposed on us is problematic. It is essentially materialistic and only allows for the recognition of the physical realm. How then do we come to know and understand the invisible realm as a knowing and knowable spirit? This is where the *Skh*, the Science of Being, requires a journey that goes beyond the boundaries of current understandings. Landing in this place of *Skh* will be and has been a collective venture where the journey of Black psychology has evolved and has continued to evolve. There comes, however, a moment in the evolutionary movement of Black psychology when the "community intelligence" of the collective wisdom of those who currently call themselves Black, African, or Pan African psychologists must recognize that the name of the science must be aligned with the nature of its be(ing), ergo, SKH. This contribution is offered as some shared thinking, perspectives, opinions, and knowledge that may serve to identify the expansion of the contours, context, and content that is driven by and is spirit, the *Skh*, the Science of Being.

While most of the time I feel I am a mystic who has a constant and immediate rapport with the divine and who is serving as a portal or channel for new and old African beingness, whatever limitations found in this contribution, I charge to my having not routinely cleansed the portal of receptivity. All else I give to the cause and the consequence of being Spirit.

What is next is for us to collectively discover.

Afterword

Martin Luther King wrote, "Where do we go from here? Chaos or community?" *Skh: From Black Psychology to the Science of Being* is the embodiment of the Association of Black Psychologists' ethical principle of courage to go from here. It exemplifies an unflinching commitment to truth, to an African worldview and episteme, and to a centering of Pan African perception, knowledge, and experience. Baba Wade Nobles has shown us the way forward, in community, guided by an African cultural worldview. More than ever, we need a road map that prioritizes that which supports and sustains our humanity and authenticity as specks of the Divine. Why do I say this? More than ever our community needs us. While we have retained many features of our African cultural foundation, we also struggle to maintain an authentic existence within which we see the value of our lives, our connection to a universal order, and our divine purpose and gift to the world. Members of our community struggle to be seen, heard, felt, and appreciated. In this struggle, some walk this world with the mantra "Born to be hated, dying to be loved"—an actual tattoo inscribed on the arm of a Boston gang member.

Ayi Kwei Armah said in his book *The Healers* that a mind here and a mind there refused to die. They refused to die under the weight of White supremacy and the lie of Black inferiority and White superiority. Instead, they chose to be healers that inspire. But how does one do that under the hegemonic weight of the White grand narrative? "Is there something we have forgotten? Some precious thing we have lost wandering in strange lands?" (Arna Bontemps). In this foreign land, "The Struggle to 'Be' is a Source of Stress" (Adams, 2015). The sage wisdom of Baba Wade Nobles is helping us to reclaim that which we have forgotten and to heal the wounds from generations in which we have struggled to be. He reminds us of the wisdom in the Yoruba proverb that "When you stand in the blessings of your mother and God, it matters not who stands against you." He enlivens the words of Frederick Douglass: "You have seen how a (wo)man was made a slave; you shall see how a slave was made a (wo)man."

Skh: From Black Psychology to the Science of Being is the embodiment of the Association of Black Psychologists' ethical principle of courage. It exemplifies an unflinching commitment to truth, to an African worldview and episteme, and to a centering of Pan African perception, knowledge, and experience. What do I mean? He speaks to *akwure*, the principle of truth. Baba Nobles boldly points the way forward, a way forward that does not defer to a Eurocentric paradigm of human existence.

The reader is invited to grapple with fundamental distinctions such as what it means to be a human being versus what is personhood. The Akan word for both human being and person is *onipa*. However, there is no vagueness or ambiguity as to which of the two meanings of *onipa* is intended in any given Akan context. When referring to a human being, the term refers to the descriptive or metaphysical components of the psychophysiological system that comprises the individuated, self-conscious being. However, human beings can hardly be considered persons until they display prescribed competencies in the discharge of moral and social responsibilities. These are the normative attributes of personhood. Such a philosophical distinction between human beingness as a condition that is bestowed and personhood as a condition that is earned is common to many sub-Saharan societies. The relationship between the two conditions is that the former is a necessary condition for the latter. *Skh: From Black Psychology to the Science of Being* calls for careful reflection of these nuances and conceptualizations of what it means to be human.

Baba Nobles grounds *Skh: From Black Psychology to the Science of Being* in African cultural thought and wisdom and historical context and instructs us to "return to the source" and explore BaNtu episteme as a conceptual grounding and by introducing culture as technology, *Skh* recommends the application of African American cultural technology as the requisite for the restorative process. He illustrates with concrete examples that our culture is our superpower, a superpower that Western neuroscience is just discerning. This is revealed through language and African science. For example, Baba Nobles unpacks the common Akan greeting, *Wohotesen* (wo-ho-te-sen), which means more than "Hello" or "How are you?" Its deeper meaning is "I lower myself before you" or "I bow down before your essence." This demonstrates that in meeting, I recognize, respect, and honor the value of your essence or Spirit, revealing the deep structure of African culture and "how" it serves as our superpower.

In *Skh: From Black Psychology to the Science of Being*, Baba Nobles has provided us with a road map for the discipline and a way to avoid reverting to White psychology by default. It is incumbent upon the current and next generation of African/Black psychologists to operationalize and apply in research and praxis the fundamental African concept that all in reality is Spirit or Energy, the meaning of being human, and the implication of the African concept of life and death. How do we move the dense set of conceptual underpinnings presented by Baba Nobles and take them to the next level of practical application?

In BaNtu philosophy, there are four categories of expression of spirit expression: (1) human beings as an expression of spirit or force; (2) place and time as expressions of spirit or force; (3) material objects like rivers, mountains, and animals; and (4) joy, beauty, laughter, love, and emotions. How do we apply these in the service of understanding, cultivating, and healing the human psyche? How do we understand and intentionally use their dynamic interplay in the service of human development and well-being? And how does this develop, wax, and wane across the lifespan? Existence is at the level of the family or peoplehood. This requires that African psychology develop community-centered strategies to support family and peoplehood.

Sometimes the revelation is presented in a single sentence dense enough to become the body of work of a doctoral dissertation or a career research trajectory. For example, there is the sentence stating, "Relationships between entities are more important than their separate identities." Sense of identity, personality theory, and habitual behavior must be reexamined.

Finally, this work flips the script on what is essential for a quality life and a quality society. The west would have us think that nations such as the United States and the United Kingdom are "first" world societies (grounded in their science, technology, GDP, and infrastructure). But what is the quality of life, happiness, and sense of connection to others among the people in these places? Places like Ghana, Senegal, and many other African countries are relegated to "third" world status because in comparison, they lag behind these Western societies (often by Western design). But the reality is that the priority given to human relations, connection to the broader realms of reality, levels of violence, psychological disorders, and loneliness are far lower. Which then is first world? It is a matter of what is valued more—people or things.

How many of us were taught the songs of the Wanyamwezi or of the Wahehe? Many of us have learned to dance the rumba, or the cha cha, to rock and roll, and to twist and even to dance the waltz and foxtrot. But how many of us can dance, or have even heard of, the *gombe sugu*, the *mangala, nyang umumi, kiduo,* or *lele mama*? Baba Nobles is returning African psychology to the *gombe sugu*, the *umumi*, the *lele mama,* and more. The word after is that *Skh: From Black Psychology to the Science of Being* is an essential guide for our going forward. In gratitude.

Cheryl Tawede Grills, PhD, Professor, Psychology
Director, Psychology Applied Research Center
President's Professor
Loyola Marymount University

Appendix

Glossary of African Language Terms and Concepts

PRELIMINARY GLOSSARY OF
AFRICAN LANGUAGE TERMINOLOGY

(Phonetic pronunciation by Dr. Vera Nobles)

Abaphansi Basifulathele (ah-bah phan-see Bah-see-foo-lah-teh-leh): Withdrawal of ancestral protection

Aidogba nínu emí (ay-doh-bah nee-noo eh-mee): Spiritual Imbalance, Imbalance in the spirit

Akom Ko (Ah-kom Koh): Without spirit

Alasal Tarey: The process through which one comes to know and understand one's origin, essence, and unfolding as a human being in order to serve humanity (Songhoy-senni)

Bulwa meso (bul-wah meh-soh): To have one's eyes open

Bwana Mboti (bwah-nah em-boh-tee): The child of my ancestors

Dikitisa (dee-kee-tee-sah): To regenerate; to renew

Dingo-dingo diandiakina: The healing process of a human being (KiKongo)

Elenini (eh-leh-nee-nee): Spirit defilement (KiKongo)

Eni Orí ę Kòpé (Eh-nee Oh-ree eh Ko-peh): He who is unable to put his mind together

Funda dia Ngolo (Foon-dah dee-ah en-goh-loh): Package of energy; the individual's self-healing power (KiKongo)

Funda dia Tambukusu (Foon-dah dee-ah Tahm-boo-koo-soo): The genetic package

139

Futu (foo-too): Everything that life has to survive. The "medicine" can be safe or dangerous

Kalunga (Kkah-loon-gah): The totality, everything, sharing life and becoming life continually after life itself. The completeness of all life. It is an ocean of energy, a force in motion. (KiKongo)

Kalunga (kah-loon-gah): The invisible wall between the physical and spiritual world

Kemba (kem-bah): To play/flirt

Kembana (kem-bah-nah): To make love

Kingongo: A state wherein the inner Divine presence is in harmony (blends) with the self-healing power (Ngolo) as expressed in all forms of being (KiKongo)

Kizungu Zungu: The defiled or damaged spirits (individual or collective) are seen as "tornadoes of the mind" or "mental chaos" (KiKongo)

Kugusa Mtima: Deals with the capacity of the collective human will via the "power" to transcend and transform human consciousness and thereby transcend ordinary existence and experience; unity with the Divine. The "touching the heart" (KiKongo)

Kumpemba (koom-pem-bah): The lower world or spiritual world

Kunseke (koon-seh-keh): The physical world of the living community

Lendo Kiandiakina (Lehn-doh Kee-ahn-dee-ah-kee-nah): Healing power

Lendo Kia Kukiniakisa (Lehn-do kee-ah Koo-kee-nee-ah-kee-sah): The self-healing power

Lendo Kia Tambikusu (Len-do kee-ah tam-bee-koo-soo): Genetic power

Loka (loh-kah): To poison or infect; to physically, mentally, and spiritually destroy

Luku: To poison or infect at a personal or community level (KiKongo)

Mayembo ma nitu (mah-yem-boh mah nee-too): Waves of energy/Electricity throughout the human body

N'kisi (Futu) (en-kee-see): To take care of; The container, as spirit force, that holds the hidden power of the mysteries of life itself

N'singa dikanda (en-seen-gah dee-kan-dah): The biogenetic rope of the communities of the dead

Ndoki (en-doh-kee): "Cause" of a thing, including illness; oppression

Nganga (en-gang'a nkisi) (en-gahn-gah En-kee-see): A powerful mediator between the visible world and the realm of spirit and ancestors. The

Healer is one capable of activating the process by which the body (persons or community) repairs, cures, or restores itself to health and well-being. The Healer cures both physical and spiritual diseases. He or she is one who restores the physical, psychic, social, and cosmic balance and harmony in and between persons, people (community), nature, and the Divine

Ngang'a nkisi (en-gahn-gah En-kee-see): The Ngang'a nkisi (Healer) is one capable of activating the process by which the body (persons or community) repairs, cures, or restores itself to health and well-being. She or he is one who restores the physical, psychic, social, and cosmic balance and harmony in and between persons, people (community), nature, and the Divine. The Ngang' nkisi (Healer) cures both physical and spiritual diseases. An Nganga serves as a powerful mediator between the visible world and the realm of spirit and ancestors

Ngolo (en-goh-loh): Energy of self-healing power (KiKongo)

Ngolo Zandiakina (En-goh-loh Zahn-dee-ah-kee-nah): Self-healing potential (KiKongo)

Nsumununu (en-soo-moo-noo-noo): When the spirit of the community and the spirit of its members become defiled or damaged.

Okan tí O bale (Oh-kahn tee Oh bah-leh): Heart unsettled

Se Alafia Ni (Shey Ah-lah-fee-ah Nee): The state of perfect and total peace

Sikere Folo (See-keh-reh Foh-loh): To act without spiritual connection

Skh Djr: Skh Djr examines and utilizes the processes that allow for the illumination and liberation of the spirit. It is an unfiltered (free of western contamination) process of understanding, examining, and explicating the meaning, nature, and functioning of being human for African people by conducting a deep, profound, and penetrating search, study, and mastery of the process of "illuminating" the human spirit or essence and totality of all human experience and phenomena

Sumuna (soo-moon-ah): Violation of self-sacredness. Sumuna is caused directly by the breaking of taboos, cultural precepts, and ancestral traditions. Community relations that violate the sacred inner self (the violation of self-sacredness) result in a state of Sumuna. Inter-, intra-, and supra-relationships can violate the sacredness of self (KiKongo)

Tambula (tahm-boo-lah): To receive sensitively

Tambudila (tahm-boo-dee-lah): To receive instrumentally

Tunda Milongi: Violation of community laws and taboos (KiKongo)

Ukugeza Umkhondo (OO-koo-geh-zah Oom-khon-doh): The cleansing of the path (especially the path where there was a violent death due to war or murder)

Ukuzilungisa (oo-koo-zee-loon-gee-sah): To heal a whole people (KiKongo-Bantu/Nguni). To remedy oneself; to heal the breakdown between oneself and the realm of the spirits

Umsebenzi (oom-seh-behn-zee): A ritual or function that is performed to appease the ancestors

Yungula (yoon-goo-lah): To pollute; to burn up

Yungulwa (yoon-gool-wah): To be polluted; burn up; brainwashed

Yurugu: Used by Marimba Ani in her African-centered critique of European thought and behavior (a self-created being born prematurely— was doomed to perpetually search for the completeness that could never be his). Forever incomplete single-souled (rather than twinned in natural and divine complementarity with the female) impure and incomplete (Dogon). Based on Dogon cosmology (Kiswahili)

Zola (**Love**): Love activates "Ngolo," the energy of self-healing power (potential). It is the undeniable desire of one's spirit to connect, merge, expand and extend into a greater oneness with another (spirit). Zola requires that one value and treasure another with caring and affection in order to sustain, promote, nurture, and inspire their "perfectibility." Zola (Love) is self and collective cherishment. It is the essential act of personal and collective preservation and actualization (Kikongo)

References

Akbar, N. (Luther X). (1974). Awareness: The key to Black mental health. *Journal of Black Psychology, 1*, 30–37.

Akbar, N. (1976). Rhythmic patterns in African personality. In L. M. King, V. J. Dixon, & W. W. Nobles (Eds.), *African philosophy: Assumptions and paradigms for research on Black persons* (pp. 176–187). Fanon Center Publications.

Akbar, N. (1979). African roots of Black personality. In W. D. Smith (Ed.), *Reflections on Black psychology* (pp. 79–87). University Press of America.

Akbar, N. (1981). Mental disorder among African Americans. *Black Books Bulletin, 7*(2), 18–25.

Akbar, N. (1985). Nile valley origins of the science of the mind. In I. V. Sertima (Ed.), *Nile valley civilizations* (pp. 13–19). Journal of African Civilization.

Akbar, N. (1990). African American consciousness and kemet: Spirituality, symbolism and duality. In M. Karenga (Ed.), *Reconstructing kemetic culture: Papers, perspectives, projects* (pp. 99–114). University of Sankore Press.

Akbar, N. (2004). *Akbar papers in African psychology*. Mind Productions & Associates.

Akbar, N. (2016). *New visions for Black men*. Mind Productions & Associates.

Akbar, N. (Published as Weems, L.). (1975). The rhythms of Black personality. *Southern Exposure, 3*, 14–19.

Akinyela, M. M. (2005). Testimony of hope: African centered praxis for therapeutic ends. *Journal of Systemic Therapies, 24*(1), 5–18.

Allen, D. F. *Advances in Black personality theory and implications for psychology*. Manuscript submitted for publication.

Ani, M. (1994). *Yurugu: An African-centered critique of European cultural thought and behavior*. African World Press.

Asante, M. K. (1980). International/Intercultural relations. In M. Asante & A. Vandi (Eds.), *Contemporary Black thought* (Chap. 3). SAGE.

Asante, M. K., & Ledbetter, C., Jr. (Eds.). (2016). *Contemporary critical thought in Africology and Africana studies*. Lexington Books.

Association of Black Psychologists. (n.d.). *Black/African-centered psychology*. https://www.abpsi.org/pdf/AfricanCenteredPsychologydefinition.pdf

Atem, K. (2006). *The book of knowing the evolutions of Ra*. Lulu Press.

Bache, M. (1895). Reaction time with reference to race. *Psychological Review, 2*, 475–586.

Baldwin, J. (1976). Black psychology and Black personality. *Black Books Bulletin, 1*(3), 6–11, 65.

Baldwin, J. (1980). *African (Black) psychology: Issues and synthesis* [Unpublished paper]. Florida A&M, Tallahassee, FL, United States.

Baldwin, J. A. (1981). Notes on an Africentric theory of Black personality. *The Western Journal of Black Studies, 5*(3), 172–79.

Baldwin, J. A. (1986, March). African (Black) psychology: Issues and synthesis. *Journal of Black Studies, 16*(3), 235–249.

Banks, W. C. (1976a). Psychohistory and the Black psychologist. *Journal of Black Psychology, 2*(2), 25–31.

Banks, W. C. (1976b). White preference in Blacks: A paradigm in search of a phenomenon. *Psychological Bulletin, 83*, 1179–86.

ben-Jochannan, Y. (1972). *Black man of the Nile and his family.* Alkebu-Lan Books.

ben-Jochannan, Y. (1972). *Cultural genocide in the Black and African Studies curriculum.* Black Classic Press.

ben-Jochannan, Y. (1991). *From the Nile Valley to the New World.* Africa World Press.

ben-Jochannan, Y. (1991). *New dimensions in African history: From the Nile Valley to the new world, science invention & technology: The London lectures of Dr. Yosef ben-Jochannan and Dr. John Henrik Clarke.* Brawtley Press.

Bentley, W. H. (1887). *Dictionary and grammar of the Kongo language: As spoken at San Salvador, the ancient capital of the Old Kongo empire, West Africa* (Vol. 1). Baptist missionary society.

Bethea, S., & Allen, T. (2013). *Past and present societal influences on African American couples that impact love and intimacy.* Routledge.

Blyden, E. W. (1869). *The Negro in ancient history.* M'Gill & Witherow (pp. 7–8).

Blyden, E. W. (1887). *Christianity, Islam and the Negro race.* Martino.

Bohm, D. (2012). *Quantum theory.* Courier Corporation.

Bojuwoye, O., & Edwards, S. (2011). Integrating ancestral consciousness into conventional counselling. *Journal of Psychology in Africa, 21*(3), 375–381.

Boring, E. G. (1929). *The history of experimental psychology.* Appleton-Century-Crofts.

Boykin, W. (1977, December). Experimental psychology from a Black perspective: Issues and answers. In W. E. Cross Jr. (Ed.), *Third conference on empirical research in Black psychology* (pp. 12–23). National Institute of Education.

Bremeister, H. (1853). *The Black man: The comparative anatomy and psychology of the African Negro.* William C. Bryant & Co., Printers.

Brooks, J. (2000). Prince Hall, Freemasonry, and genealogy. *African American Review, 34*(2), 197–216.

Brown, W. W. (1863). *The Black man: His antecedents, his genius, and his achievements.* James Redpath.

Bruce, J. E. (1899). *Concentration of energy: Bruce uses plain language in emphasizing the power of organization.* Unknown publisher.

Bruce, J. E. (1901). *The blood red record.* Argus Company, Printers.

Bruce, J. E. (1907–1909). *The Black sleuth* [Serial]. McGirt's Magazine.

Bruce, J. E. (1910). *Eminent Negroes.* Unknown publisher.

Bruce, J. E. (1921). *Prince Hall, the pioneer of Negro Masonry: Proofs of the legitimacy of Prince Hall Masonry.* Hunt Printing.

Bruce, J. E. (n.d.). *The blot of the scutcheon.* Unknown publisher.

Bruce, J. E. (n.d.). *No heaven for the Black man.* Unknown publisher.

Budge, E. (1997). *An introduction to ancient Egyptian literature.* Dover Publications.

Budge, E. W. (1981). *An Egyptian hieroglyphic dictionary.* Рипол Классик.

Churchward, A. (1978). *The signs and symbols of primordial man.* Greenward Press.

Clark, C. X., McGee, D. P., Nobles, W., & Weems, L. X. (1975). Voodoo or IQ: An introduction to African psychology. *Journal of Black Psychology, 1*(2), 9–20.

Clark, K. (1965). *Dark Ghetto.* Harper & Row.

Clarke, J. H. (1940, September). Boy who painted Christ black. *Opportunity: A Journal of Negro Life, 18*(9), 264–266.

Clarke, J. H. (1976). African cultural continuity and slave revolts in the new world: Part one. *The Black Scholar, 8*(1), 41–49.

Clarke, J. H. (1990). *The African world revolution* (2nd ed.). Africa World Press.

Clarke, J. H. (1992). *Africa, lost and found with Richard More and Keith Baird; Notes for an African world: Africans at the crossroads.* Africa World Press.

Clarke, J. H. (1992). *Christopher Columbus and the African holocaust.* EWorld.

Clarke, J. H. (1993). *Who betrayed the African Revolution* (2nd. ed.). Third World Press.

Clarke, J. H. (1999). *My life in search of Africa.* Third World Press.

Clegg, B. (2019). *Dark matter and dark energy: The hidden 95% of the universe.* Icon Books.

Constantine, M. G., Okazaki, S., & Utsey, S. O. (2004). Self-concealment, social self-efficacy, acculturative stress, and depression in African, Asian, and Latin American international college students. *American Journal of Orthopsychiatry, 74*(3), 230–241.

Cross, W. E., Jr. (1971, July). The Negro-to-Black conversion experience: Toward a psychology of lack Liberation. *Black World,* (20)9, 13–27.

Dawkins, R. (1989). *The selfish gene* (2nd ed.). Oxford University Press.

Delaney, M. R. (1879). *Principia of ethnology: The origin of races and color.* Harper & Brother.

Diop, C. A. (1974). *The African origins of civilization: Myth or reality.* Lawrence Hill.

Diop, C. A. (1989). *The cultural unity of Black Africa: The domains of patriarchy and of matriarchy in classical antiquity.* Karnak House.

Diop, C. A. (1991). *Civilization and barbarism* (3rd ed.). Lawrence Hill Books. (Originally published 1981)

Diop, C. A. (1988). *Precolonial Black Africa* (7th ed.). Lawrence Hill Books.

Dixon, V. J. (1976). World views and research methodology. In L. M. King, V. J. Dixon, & W. W. Nobles (Eds.), *African philosophy: Assumptions and paradigms for research on Black persons.* Fanon Research and Development Center Publications.

Dompere, K. K. (2006). *Polyrhythmicity: Foundations of African philosophy.* Adonis & Abbey.

Du Bois, W. E. B. (2007). *Dusk of dawn: An essay toward an autobiography of a race concept: The oxford WEB Du Bois* (Vol. 8). Oxford University Press.

Du Bois, W. E. B., & Marable, M. (2015). *Souls of Black folk.* Routledge.

Dzobo, N. K. (1992). African symbols and proverbs as sources of knowledge. In K. Wiredu, & K. Gyekye (vol. 1). CRVP Series II.

Easton, H. (1837). *A treatise on the intellectual character & civil and political condition of the colored people of the United States: And the prejudice exercised towards them.* I. Knapp.

Ehret, C. (2001). Bantu expansions: Re-envisioning a central problem of early African history. *International Journal of African Historical Studies, 34,* 5–41.

Epstein, E. L., & Kole, R. (Eds.). (1998). *The language of African literature.* Africa World Press.

Fanon, F. (1988). *Toward the African revolution: Political essays.* Grove Press.

Fanon, F. (2004). *The wretched of the Earth* (R. Philcox, Trans.; 6.). Grove Press. (Original work published 1961)

Fanon, F. (2008). *Black skin, white masks.* Grove Press.

Fanon, F. (2022). *A dying colonialism.* Grove/Atlantic.

Ferguson, G. O., Jr. (1916). *The psychology of the Negro: An experimental study.* The Science Press.

Ferris, W. H. (1913). *The African abroad: Or, his evolution in western civilization, tracing his development under Caucasian milieu* (Vol. 2). Johnson Reprint Corporation.

Finch, C. S. (1998). *The star of deep beginnings: The genesis of African sciences and technology.* Khenti.

Freud, S., & Strachey, J. E. (1964). *The standard edition of the complete psychological works of Sigmund Freud.* Hogarth Press.

Friend-du-Preez, N., Cameron, N., & Griffiths, P. (2009). Stuips, spuits and prophet ropes: The treatment of abantu childhood illnesses in urban South Africa. *Social Science & Medicine, 68*(2), 343–351.

Fu-Kiau, K. K. B. (1991). *Self-healing power and therapy-old teachings from Africa.* Vantage Press.

Fu-Kiau, K. K. B. (2001). *Tying the spiritual knot: African cosmology of the Bantu-Kongo* (2nd ed.). Athelia Henrietta Press.

Galton, F. (1869). *Hereditary genius: Its laws and consequences.* MacMillan.

Goddard, L., Rowe, D. M., McInnis, E. M., & DeLoach, C. (2020). The role of proverbs in African-centred psychology. *Alternation, 27*(1), 224–243.

Grier, W. H., & Cobbs, P. M. (1968). *Black rage.* Bantam Books.

Grills, C. (2002). African-centered psychology: Basic principles. In T. A. Parham (Ed.), *Counseling persons of African descent: Raising the bar of practitioner competence* (pp. 10–24). SAGE.

Grills, C., Nobles, W. W., & Hill, C. (2018). African, Black, neither or both? Models and strategies developed and implemented by The Association of Black Psychologists. *Journal of Black Psychology, 44*(8), 791–826.

Grills, C., & Rowe, D. (1996). African traditional medicine: Implications for African centered approaches to healing. In R. Jones (Ed.), *Advances in African American psychology: Theory, paradigms and research* (pp. 71–100). Cobb & Henry.

Guthrie, R. V. (1976). *Even the rat was white.* Harper & Row.

Guthrie, R. V. (2004). *Even the rat was white* (2nd ed.). Pearson.

Gyekye, K. (1997). *Tradition and modernity: Philosophical reflections on the African experience.* Oxford University Press.

Hall, C. S. (1954). *A primer of Freudian psychology.* World Publishing.

Hall, S. G. (1905). The Negro in Africa and America. *Pedagogical Seminary, 12,* 350–368.

Hansberry, L., & J. E. Harris (Ed.). (1981). *Africa and Africans: As seen by classical writers.* Howard University Press.

Harrell, S. P. (2015). Culture, wellness, and world "PEaCE": An introduction to person-environment-and-culture-emergence theory. *Community Psychology in Global Perspective, 1*(1), 16–49.

Harris, W. T., & Sawyer, H. (1968). *The springs of Mende belief and conduct: A discussion of the influence of the belief in the supernatural among the Mende.* Sierra Leone University Press.

Higgins, C., Jr. (1994). *Feeling the spirit.* Bantam.

Hilliard, A. (1978, June 20). "Anatomy and dynamics of oppression," An address delivered at the First National Conference on Human Relations in Education, Minneapolis, MN.

Hilliard, A. (1981). I.Q. as catechism: Ethnic and cultural bias or invalid science. *Black Books Bulletin, 7*(2), 99–112.

Hilliard, A. (1983, August). I.Q. and the Courts' Larry P. vs. Wilson Riles and Pase vs. Hannon. *Journal of Black Psychology, 10*(1), 1–19.

Hindess, B. (1996). *Discourses of power: From Hobbes to Foucault.* Wiley-Blackwell.

Holly, J. T. (1857). *A vindication of the capacity of the negro race for self-government, and civilized progress: As demonstrated by historical events of the Haytian revolution; and the subsequent acts of that people since their national independence.* WH Stanley, Printer.

Houston, D. D. (2013). *The wonderful Ethiopians of the ancient Cushite empire, Book I: Nations of the Cushite empire, marvelous facts from authentic records, wonderful Ethiopians.* Universal Publishing. (Originally published 1926)

Jackson, G. (1979). The origin and development of Black psychology: Implications for Black Studies and Human Behaviour. *Studies Africaine, 1*(3), 271–292.

Jackson, J. G. (2015). *Introduction to African civilizations.* Ravenio Books.

James, G. (1976). *Stolen legacy.* Julian Richardson Associates

Jamison, D. F. (2018). Key concepts, theories, and issues in African/Black psychology: A view from the bridge. *Journal of Black Psychology, 44*(8), 722–746.

Jenkins, A. H. (1982). *The psychology of the Afro-American: A humanistic approach.* Pergamon Press.

Jones, R. L. (Ed.). (1972). *Black psychology.* Harper & Row.

Jung, C. G. (1950). Lecture to Zurich Psychoanalytic Society in 1912, reprinted as "On the Psychology of the Negro." In W. McGuire (Ed.), *Collected works of Carl G. Jung* (Vol. 18, pp. 29, 552). Princeton University Press.

Kagame, A. (1989). The problem of "man" in Bantu philosophy. *Journal of African Religion and Philosophy, 1,* 35–40.

Karenga, M. (1993). *Introduction to Black studies* (2nd ed.). University of Sankore Press.

Karenga, M. (2004). *Maat, the moral ideal in ancient Egypt: A study in classical African ethics.* Psychology Press.

Karenga, M., & Carruthers, J. H. (1986). *Kemet and the African Worldview: Research, rescue and restoration.* University of Sankore.

Khatib, S. (1980). Black studies and the study of Black people: Reflections on the distinctive characteristics of Black psychology. In R. Jones (Ed.), *Black psychology* (2nd ed., pp. 48–55). Harper & Row.

King, L. (1976). On the nature of a creative world: Toward the restoration of creativity in psychology. In L. M. King, V. J. Dixon, & W. W. Nobles (Eds.), *African philosophy: Assumptions and paradigms for research on Black persons*. Fanon Research and Development Center.

King, L. (1980). Models of meaning in mental health: Model eight—The transformation of the oppressed. *Fanon Center Journal, 1*(1), 9–49.

King, R. (1982). Black dot, black seed: The archetype of humanity. *Uraeus, 2*(3), 4–22.

Lewis, R. B. (1844): *Light and truth*. Benjamin F. Roberts, Printer.

Logan, R. W. (1936). *The African background outlined, or handbook for the study of the Negro*. Association for the Study of Negro Life and History.

Maiga, H. O. (1996). *Conversational Sonay language of Mali*. Albarka International.

Malklaka, L. (2015). *Holographic sub-quantum mind*. Author.

Mayers, S. (1976). Intuitive synthesis in ebonies: Implications for a developing African science. In L. M. King, V. J. Dixon, & W. W. Nobles (Eds.), *African philosophy: Assumptions and paradigms for research on Black persons* (pp. 190–214). Fanon Center Publications.

Mazama, A. (2021). Africology and the question of disciplinary language. *Journal of Black Studies, 52*(5), 447–464.

Mbiti, J. S. (1970). *African religion and philosophy*. Heinemann Educational Books.

Mbiti, J. S. (1990). *African religions and philosophy* (2nd ed.). Heinemann Educational Books.

Mkhize, N. (2004). Psychology: An African. In N. Duncan, K. Ratele, D. Hook, N. Mkhize, P. Kiguwa, & A. Collins (Eds.), *Self, community and psychology* (pp. 24–52). UCT Press.

Moses, W. J. (2008). Africa and Pan-Africanism in the thought of Du Bois. In S. Zamir (Ed.), *The Cambridge companion to W. E. B. Du Bois* (pp. 117–130). Cambridge University Press.

Myers, L. (1981). *Oneness: A Black model of psychological functioning*. Paper presented at the 14th Annual Convention of the Association of Black Psychologists, Denver, CO, August 1981.

Nagel, E. (1961). *The structure of science: Problems in the logic of scientific explanation* (Vol. 1, p. 474). Harcourt, Brace & World.

Nardal, P. (1929). Feminism and L'Internationalisme Noir. In B. H. Edwards (Ed.), *The practice of diaspora* (pp. 119–186). Harvard University Press.

Ngubane, H. (1976). Aspects of Zulu treatment. *Social Anthropology and Medicine*. London.

Ngubane, J. K. (1979). *Conflict of minds: Changing power is position in South Africa*. Books in Focus.

Ngubane, S. (2012). Death and burial practices in contemporary Zulu culture. *Mankind Quarterly, 53*(1), 91.

Nobles, W. (1974). African root and American fruit: The Black family. *Journal of Social and Behavioral Sciences, 20*(2), 52–63.

Nobles, W. W. (1976). Extended-self: Rethinking the so-called Negro self-concept. *Journal of Black Psychology, 2*(2), 15–24.

Nobles, W. W. (1978). The archeology of the African spirit: Toward a deeper discourse. *Journal of Black Studies*. San Francisco State University.

Nobles, W. W. (1980). African philosophy: Foundations of Black psychology. In R. L. Jones (Ed.), *Black psychology* (2nd ed., pp. 23–36). Harper & Row.

Nobles, W. W. (1986a). *African psychology: Toward its reclamation, reascension and revitalization*. A Black Family Institute Publication.

Nobles, W. W. (1986b). Ancient Egyptian thought and the development of African (Black) psychology. In M. Karenga & J. H. Carruthers (Eds.), *Kemet and the African worldview* (pp. 110–118). University of Sankore Press.

Nobles, W. W. (1995). *Touching the spirit: Success for African American students*. Professional Development Institute Training Manual, Oakland, CA.

Nobles, W. W. (1997). To be African or not to be: The question of identity or authenticity—some preliminary thoughts. In R. L. Jones (Ed.), *African American identity development: Theory, research, and intervention* (pp. 203–213). Cobb & Henry.

Nobles, W. W. (2006). *Seeking the Sakhu: Foundational writings for an African psychology*. Third World Press.

Nobles W. W. (2007). *Shattered consciousness & fractured identity: The lingering psychological effects of the transatlantic slave trade experience* (Final Report). Illinois Transatlantic Slave Trade Commission.

Nobles W. W. (2012). *The Island of Memes: Haiti's contradictory cache of consciousness—The unfinished revolution*. Black Classical Press.

Nobles, W. W. (2013). Shattered consciousness, fractured identity: Black psychology and the restoration of the African psych. *Journal of Black Psychology*, *39*(3), 232–242. https://jbp.sagepub.com

Nobles, W. W. (2015). From Black psychology to Sakhu Djr: Implications for the further development of a Pan African Black psychology. *Journal of Black Psychology*, *41*(5), 399–414.

Nobles, W. W., Baloyi, L., & Sodi, T. (2016). Pan African humanness and *sakhu djaer* as praxis for indigenous knowledge systems. *Alternation Special Edition*, *18*.

Nobles, W., Goddard, L., & Watson, S. (2017). *African American holistic wellness hub complex, research and planning design initiative*. Final Report, ACBHCS Contract # 900460, Oakland, CA.

Obasi, E. M., Flores, L. Y., & James-Myers, L. (2009). Construction and initial validation of the Worldview Analysis Scale (WAS). *Journal of Black Studies*, *39*(6), 937–961. https://doi.org/10.1177/0021934707305411

Obasi, E. M., & Leong, F. T. (2009). Psychological distress, acculturation, and mental health-seeking attitudes among people of African descent in the United States: A preliminary investigation. *Journal of Counseling Psychology*, *56*(2), 227.

Obenga, T. (1992). *Ancient Egypt and Black Africa: A student's handbook for the study of Ancient Egypt in philosophy, linguistics, and gender relations*. Karnak House.

Obenga, T. (Ed.). (1995). *Readings in precolonial central Africa: Texts & documents*. Red Sea Press.

Obenga, T. (1998). *African Philosophy in World History*. Sungai.

Obenga, T. (2004). *African philosophy: The pharaonic period, 2780–330 BC*. Per Ankh.

Ojelade, I. I., McCray, K., Meyers, J., & Ashby, J. (2014). Use of indigenous African healing practices as a mental health intervention. *Journal of Black Psychology, 40*(6), 491–519.

Opoku, K. A. (1978). *West African traditional religion.* FEP International Private Limited.

Owuso-Bempah, J., & Howitt, D. (1995). How Eurocentric psychology damages Africa. *The Psychologist, 7,* 163–166.

Parham, T. A. (2002). *Counseling persons of African descent: Raising the bar of practitioner competence.* SAGE.

Parham, T. A., Ajamu, A., & White, J. L. (2015). *Psychology of Blacks: Centering our perspectives in the African consciousness.* Psychology Press.

Pennington, J. W. (1841). *A text book of the origin and history, etc., of the colored people.* Negro History Press.

Perry, R. L. (1893). *The Cushite, or, the descendants of Ham: As found in the sacred scriptures and in the writings of ancient historians and poets from Noah to the Christian Era.* Willey & Company.

Piper-Mandy, E., & Rowe, T. D. (2010). Educating African-Centered psychologists: Towards a comprehensive paradigm. *Journal of Pan African Studies, 3*(8), 5–23.

Rabaka, R. (2006). Africana critical theory of contemporary society: The role of radical politics, social theory, and Africana philosophy. In M. K. Asante & M. Karenga (Eds.), *Handbook of Black studies* (pp. 130–151). SAGE.

Rabaka, R. (2010). *Africana critical theory: Reconstructing the Black radical tradition, from WEB Du Bois and CLR James to Frantz Fanon and Amilcar Cabral.* Lexington Books.

Rabaka, R. (2015). *The Negritude movement.* Rowman & Littlefield.

Ramose, M. B. (2002). *African philosophy through Ubuntu.* Mond Brooks.

Rogers, J. A. (2009). *World's great men of color: Volume II.* Recording for the Blind & Dyslexic.

Rowe, D. M., & Webb-Msemaji, F. (2004). African-centered psychology in the community. In R. Jones (Ed.), *Black Psychology* (pp. 701–721). Cobb & Henry.

Schomburg, A. (1925). The Negro digs up his past. In A. Locke (Ed.), *The new Negro: An interpretation* (pp. 231–237). Albert and Charles Boni.

Smith, E. (2020). *Quantum physics for beginners: The ultimate guide to discover the secrets of quantum mechanics, understand essential theories like the theory of relativity, and the entanglement theory.* Author.

Sow, I. (1980). *Anthropological structures of madness in Black Africa.* International University Press.

Spencer, H. (1896). *The principles of psychology.* Appleton-Century-Crofts.

Strachey, J. (1953). *The standard edition of the complete psychological works of Sigmund Freud.* Hogarth Press.

Tang, R., & Dai, J. (2014). Biophoton signal transmission and processing in the brain. *Journal of Photochemistry and Photobiology, 139,* 71–75. doi: 0.1016/j.jphotbiol.2013.12.008

Thomas, L. V. (1961). Time, myth and history in West Africa. *Presence' Africaine, 11*(39), 50–92.

Thorndike, E. L. (1940). *Human nature and the social order.* Macmillan.

Tushini, N. (2011). *An exploration of the therapeutic value of Ihlambo: Community members' perspectives* [Doctoral dissertation]. University of KwaZulu-Natal, Durban, South Africa. http://hdl.handle.net/10413/5014

Tyson, N. D. (2004, November). The importance of being constant. *Natural History.*

Vastey, P. V. (1823). *An essay on the causes of the revolution & civil wars in Haiti.* Western Luminary Office.

Viriri, A., & Mungwini, P. (2010). African cosmology and the duality of western hegemony: The search for an African identity. *The Journal of Pan African Studies, 3*(6), 27–42.

Walker, D. (1840). *Walker's appeal in four articles.* Author.

White, J. L. (1984). *The psychology of Blacks: An Afro-American perspective.* Prentice Hall.

White, J., & Thomas P. (1990). *The psychology of Blacks: An African American perspective.* Prentice Hall.

Wilcox, R. C. (1971). *The psychological consequences of being a Black American.* Wiley.

Williams, B. H. (1997). *Coming together: The founding of the association of Black psychologists* [Dissertations]. Saint Louis University. (UMI No. 9822882).

Williams, C. (1974). The destruction of Black civilization [Book Review]. *Negro History Bulletin, 38*(1), 339.

Williams, C. (1961). *Rebirth of African civilization.* Brawtley Press.

Williams, G. W. (1882). *History of the Negro race in America from 1619 to 1880: Negroes as slaves, as soldiers, and as citizens; Together with a preliminary consideration of the unity of the human family, an historical sketch of Africa, and an account of the Negro governments of Sierra Leone and Liberia* (Vol. 2). GP Putnam's Sons.

Williams, R. L. (1975). *Ebonics: The true language of Black folks.* Institute of Black Studies.

Williams, R. L. (2008). *History of the Association of Black Psychologists: Profiles of outstanding Black psychologists.* AuthorHouse.

Wilson, A. S. (1993). The falsification of African consciousness: Eurocentric history, psychiatry and the politics of White supremacy. Afrikan World Infosystems.

Woodson, C. G. (2023). *The mis-education of the Negro.* Penguin. (Original work published 1933)

Index

About the Author

Baba Dr. Wade Ifágbemì Sàngódáre Nobles is the great, great, great-grandson of Candace/Agnes, an enslaved African, born in 1810 on the Cook Plantation in Edgefield, South Carolina. Baba Dr. Wade is the namesake of Agnes's oldest son, Wade, born in 1836, who was also enslaved in South Carolina. Through mitochondrial DNA testing, Baba Wade belongs to the Temne people of Sierra Leone. Along with his wife, Dr. Vera Lynn Winmilawe Nokwanda DeMoultrie, whose mitochondrial DNA identifies her ancestry from the Jola people of Senegal, they have five children (Michael Chikuya, Omar Jahmal, Zetha Awura, Ayanna Yasmeen, and Halima Bisa) and thirteen grandchildren (Talia, Mikal, Kristofer, Donovan, Johnathan, Deborah, Maasai, Afolarin, Moremi, Folasade, Yasmeen, Oni Chinyere, Zane Nicholas). Baba Dr. Wade Ifágbemì Sàngódáre Nobles was initiated into the IFA spiritual system of Nigeria by Baba Araba Ifayemi Eleibuibon; enstooled as the Nkousohene (development subchief) by Nana Keseku I and the elders of Akwasiho, Ghana; and recognized by Baba Credo Mutwa, the High Sanusi of South Africa as a two-headed lion with one head in Africa and one head in America. Baba Nobles is considered one of the leading architects in the development of the discipline of Black psychology in the United States. For over 50 years, he has studied classical African philosophy (Kemet, Twa, and Nubian) and traditional African wisdom traditions (Akan, Yoruba, Bantu, Wolof, Kongo, Dogon, Fon, Lebou, etc.) as the grounding for the development of an authentic Black psychology. Baba Dr. Wade is cofounder and past president of the Association of Black Psychologists; the founder and former executive director of the Institute for the Advanced Study of Black Family Life and Culture; and professor emeritus (retired) in the Department of Africana (Black) Studies, at San Francisco State University. Baba Dr. Nobles is the author of over 100 articles, chapters, research reports, and books; the coauthor of the seminal article in Black psychology, *Voodoo or IQ: An Introduction to African Psychology;* and the author of *Seeking the Sakhu: Foundational Writings in African Psychology*, an anthology of over 30 years of African-centered research and scholarship. His newest manuscript, *The Island of Memes: Haiti's Unfinished Revolution,* was described by

Dr. Theophile Obenga as perhaps the most important book of the last five decades. Baba Dr. Nobles has lectured in Ghana, South Africa, England, Haiti, and Cuba and served as a visiting professor in Salvador de Bahia and São Paulo in Brazil. His professional career as a teacher, researcher, academician, and scholar has been a consistent and formal engagement in the on-going theoretical development and programmatic application of African (Black) psychology, *Skh Tm,* African-centered thought, and cultural-grounded scholarship to address the liberation and restoration of the African mind and worldwide development of African people. Dr. Nobles states, "While I think I have spent my entire life seeking an understanding of African and African American history, culture, philosophy, and spirituality, in actuality, I have been pulled and directed by a constant and immediate rapport with the invisible realm and the *Badimo* (dwellers in heaven). I am a seeker of the *Skh* (illumination) because the African spirit is constantly with me and continuously directs my path and purpose."

A Note on the Cover

The Adinkra symbols on the cover were the chosen symbolic motif of the Institute for the Advanced Study of Black Family Life and Culture, Inc. (circa 1980) that, in devoting itself to the mission of understanding and elevating Black family, life, and culture, as an organization, would always seek to find and embrace interdependence, harmony, unity, community, perseverance, strength, wisdom, and endurance.

Gye Nyame means "except God." It expresses the ominpotence and supremacy of God in all affairs.

Aya means "fern." It is a symbol of endurance, independence, defiance against difficulties, hardiness, perseverance, and resourcefulness.

Bi Nka Bi means "Nobody should bite another." It is a symbol of justice, fair play, freedom, peace, forgiveness, unity, harmony, and the avoidance of conflict or strife.

Nkonsonkonson means "chain." It is a symbol of unity and community.

Nyame Nwu Na Mawu means "God won't die for me to die." It is a symbol expressing the immortality of the human soul, expressing faith in God to preserve one's soul.

Dweninmmen means "the horns of a ram." It represent strength (in mind, body, and soul), humility, wisdom, and learning.

Hwehwemudua means "rod of investigation," that is, a measuring rod. It is a symbol of excellence, superior quality, perfection, knowledge, and critical examination.